"*Intimate Wisdom, The Sacred Art of Love* offers a new pa
intimacy. This is a unique resource for healthy sexuality and healthy relationships."
— Riane Eisler, author of *The Chalice and the Blade* and *Sacred Pleasure*

"Karinna weaves a tapestry of the most important traditions of intimacy into a coherent and sensitive reflection on the power of love."
— Timothy Dobbins, Episcopal Priest and author of *Stepping Up: Make Decisions that Matter*

"LOVE is the most powerful emotion one can express. ***In Intimate Wisdom: The Sacred Art of Love***, Karinna has provided the ultimate guide to reveal how to express and experience love at the deepest level."
— Peggy McColl, New York Times Best Selling Author of Your Destiny Switch

Karinna Kittles-Karsten here offers at once a system which unifies body and soul, mind and heart, lover and lover, achieving wholeness and oneness in the context of a sensual and impassioned spirituality from which we all can greatly benefit.
— M. Daniel Nienaltow, M.D., C.M., Columbia University & private psychiatric practice, NYC

"*Intimate Wisdom* reminds us that true love is a deeply spiritual connection between people from the depths of their hearts and lives and that The Sacred Art of Love is based on trust, not technique. I highly recommend this book."
— Rabbi Stan Levy, Los Angeles, Calif

"If you are ready to discover how the time honored love secrets of the East can create a profoundly positive effect on your love life, read this book. For Intimate Wisdom is sure to add great health, pleasure and meaning to your love life."
— MANTAK CHIA, Author of The Multi-Orgasmic Couple and Founder of The International Healing Tao Association.

"Intimate Wisdom is uplifting, sensual, and inspiring. It vibrates with the truth about sexuality and spirituality."
— Christiane Northrup, MD, author of *Mother-Daughter Wisdom* (Bantam, 2005), *The Wisdom of Menopause* (Bantam, revised 2006), and *Women's Bodies, Women's Wisdom* (Bantam, revised 2006)

Intimate Wisdom

Intimate Wisdom

The Sacred Art of Love

Karinna Kittles-Karsten

iUniverse, Inc.

New York Lincoln Shanghai

Intimate Wisdom
The Sacred Art of Love

iUniverse books may be ordered through booksellers or by contacting:

iUniverse
2021 Pine Lake Road, Suite 100
Lincoln, NE 68512
www.iuniverse.com
1-800-Authors (1-800-288-4677)

Because of the dynamic nature of the Internet, any Web addresses or links contained in this book may have changed since publication and may no longer be valid.

The views expressed in this work are solely those of the author and do not necessarily reflect the views of the publisher, and the publisher hereby disclaims any responsibility for them.

Illustrations by Armando Torellini—theCUBEexperiment

ISBN: 978-0-595-41957-9 (pbk)
ISBN: 978-0-595-86297-9 (ebk)

Printed in the United States of America

Contents

Acknowledgments

I want to express my gratitude and love to the people who have supported me as I brought this book to fruition.

First and foremost, I want to thank my husband and partner, Timothy, whose deep love and amazing spirit inspire me every day.

To my book editor, Melissa Pilgrim, thank you for all the incredible and thoughtful work, time and dedication you gave to this book. To David Andrusia, who sculpted the proposal for the book, thank you very much. To Peter Stranger, thank you for the beautiful photograph you took for the book jacket.

I want to thank all my teachers, with special thanks to Master Mantak Chia, Master Li Jun Feng, and Riane Eisler, who have shared their tremendous knowledge with me, enriching my life and work.

I also want to thank those whom I have had the opportunity to love and who have loved me. These experiences have brought forth my most needed lessons and growth.

And lastly, I want to thank my mother, Victoria, my father, Peter, my step parents Tim and Nassrin, and all my family and friends for their faith, vision, and love.

Preface

Ever since I can remember, I've been on a path to discover Sacred Love. I began this journey as a seven-year-old child of divorce full of emotional inquiry and who often displayed ample sexual energy that wasn't appropriate in a loving, devout Christian household in the South. I passed through my parents' divorce, the introduction of a stepparent, and the onset of hormones without understanding anything about intimacy. As a result, I gravitated to the only education on intimacy and relationships I could easily find—*General Hospital*. There I discovered Luke and Laura and Anna and Scorpio, who had rather complex, dramatic relationships with each other that were, above all, highly sexual. This was in stark contrast and much more interesting than my weekly Sunday school education where lessons on resisting the sinful temptation of sex were drilled in. By high school, I couldn't wait to finally free myself from my confusion about intimacy and find out for myself what love and sex were really all about.

My first discoveries of love and sexuality soon unfolded underneath the lights and glamour of my early adulthood as a fashion model working in New York, Europe, and Asia. I traveled to exotic, mystical Eastern countries, including Japan, Thailand, Hong Kong, and Taiwan. I also lived and worked in countries of legendary romance—Italy, Spain, and France—all before I was twenty-four years old. Experiencing the world on such a grand scale at a young age was profoundly eye opening and formative. I drank in the culture, the art, and the sensuality of these places. Being young and romantic, I fell in love several times and was fascinated to observe and experience for myself how people love and make love differently around the world.

As my life experiences grew and deepened, I began to look not only at the romantic connections I was making but also at the meaning in my relationship experiences. My desire to understand my own relationship with love and sex has taken me to incredible heights and heartbreaking lows—and the lows have been akin to visits that ancient Greek myths refer to as "the underworld." I am not alone in taking this kind of journey; many people do. And it can either crush us or, as I have found, develop our greatest strengths.

My formal and yet nontraditional education of what I now call "Sacred Love" began quite unassumingly. While living in New York, I was introduced to a Chinese master of ancient Taoist arts by a friend. Little did I know that this intriguing introduction would not only answer some of my ever-present inquiries about intimacy but would also lead to my life's work.

During my first weekend of study, the teacher, Master Mantak Chia, taught the concept and practice of integrating sexuality with spirit. The realization that I could potentially transcend my long-ingrained, dichotomous way of thought and behavior about sex and spirituality was a true moment of awakening for me. This powerful concept began rewiring my psyche, and soon my relationship to love, sex, and intimacy was forever altered. I launched into many more years of intensive study of both Eastern and Western intimacy methodologies and undertook demanding certification processes. I became a Certified Taoist Educator specializing in teaching the Chinese Art of Love through The Healing Tao Institute of America in New York and The International Healing Tao Association based in Chiang Mai, Thailand.

During this intensive development period, I also wrestled with integrating the principles I was learning in my studies into my own experiences in intimate relationships.

One of my first big lessons was developing a healthy communication style during conflict. Whenever I had a fight with a boyfriend, I would walk out of the room—or worse, threaten to leave the relationship altogether. I found myself feeling vulnerable, and my actions were a weak attempt to regain control. Through my studies of the Art of Love, I learned how to stay centered during a chaotic situation by connecting to and slowing down my breath and movements. This one lesson helped me stay present and regain my ability to communicate in a healthy way during a relationship conflict. I experienced immediate results, such as greater calmness and confidence, which flowed through the tone of my voice. Then, with more practice, I was able to choose words more consciously, and my impulse to leave the room diminished. My commitment to this ongoing practice continues to reward me with few communication conflicts.

Another challenge, one of my greatest, was identifying what qualities I needed in a partner to share real compatibility in a relationship. I found myself choosing relationship partners based on one or two big relationship needs, such as sexual fulfillment or mental compatibility. While those areas of the relationship flourished, other important areas were abandoned or agonizingly fought over all the time. Though I experienced several relationships that failed, over time my commitment to my psychological studies and meditative practices brought forth the personal realizations that would heal. Most significantly, I discovered that to create relationship success, I needed to share a relationship that had multiple dimensions, which included emotional, physical, mental, and spiritual compatibility. Only by having all four of these key areas present did I begin to experience a relationship that fostered an overall sense of health, wholeness, and the potential for growth. This occurred in meeting and developing the wonderful relationship I enjoy today with my husband, Timothy.

These lessons, learned from my intimacy education, served me in my own life and also in helping others.

Once I integrated the understanding and the practice of intimate wisdom, I began teaching in private practice and giving presentations at such prestigious institutions as New York University, subsequently on television shows like NBC's *Starting Over*, and in the pages of national magazines like *Self*.

The ideas and skills presented in *Intimate Wisdom* are drawn from my discoveries, experiences, and many years working as a teacher. They are meant as a map to guide you, inspire you, and help you avoid love's pitfalls in order to create a truly intimate relationship that will offer you fulfillment and the freedom to be all that you can be, a relationship that nurtures wholeness, health, ecstasy, individuality, and sacred union.

Introduction

What You Will Discover In This Book

Is it possible to find true love?
How can I attract the right partner?
How can I resolve the challenges I face again and again in my relationship?
Is sustaining a passionate, fulfilling relationship realistic?

These are some of the questions I will help you answer within this book.

Intimate Wisdom includes three parts: The Sacred Lover, The Talent of Loving Another, and The Art of Sacred Love-Making. Each part offers intimacy wisdom from the East and West, with specific exercises to help you create your ultimate intimate relationship. This book is intended for individuals who are seeking a great intimate relationship as well as for couples who want to make their current relationship even better. Skills in Part One can be practiced alone or with a partner. Talents in Part Two and Arts in Part Three are intended for practice with a partner.

I suggest that you utilize a journal to achieve maximum results from this book. You can make a journal entry after you read through a new concept and you want to write down your thoughts about it. You can also use your journal to do the exercises mentioned in the book.

An example of a journal entry could be: "I am reading Accepting Yourself and Inviting Great Love to Enter Your Life under Skill One. This is bringing up some old feelings for me.... I have decided I want to focus on accepting myself more and letting go of my self-criticism. I am going to start by creating a fun way to express my whole body by finally planting my garden today."

Throughout the book, you will be introduced to skills, then talents, and finally arts to help build your progression in your discovery and development of Intimate Wisdom.

In Part One: The Sacred Lover, you will learn *skills* to nurture and develop the lover within yourself by opening up more fully to the love and intimacy you want. You will also explore the ancient sages' use of sex as sacred artistry (and discover how you can too). In addition, you will learn how to recognize and attract your Sacred Lover.

In Part Two: The Talent of Loving Another, you will develop the *talents* for having and sustaining a passionate, healthy, and loving relationship. You will learn the talent of creating a meaningful, intimate connection with your loved one that will nurture both of you emotionally, physically, mentally, and spiritually. Then you will be exposed to a variety of innovative ways to successfully communicate with your partner. You will also learn how you can quickly achieve a more dynamic and gratifying relationship any time you need.

In Part Three: The Art of Sacred Love-Making, I offer this new term, Sacred Love-Making to describe a new and meaningful way to experience and celebrate sexual union. You will be introduced to ancient sexual intimacy *arts* that will allow you to enjoy greater passion with your Sacred Lover. You will discover how to fashion a harmonious and sacred space for intimacy. You will learn how to experience ongoing sexual chemistry with your partner. And then you will find out how to bring these principles alive in your bedroom and beyond by exploring erotic love play, secret ecstatic lovemaking methods, natural and wild sexual positions, as well as ways to experience sacred union every time you make love.

This book is a journey of love, of finding love within you, of working through the challenges and trials and disappointments of love, and of learning how to become a Sacred Lover—a lover who is confident, open-hearted, and skilled in the intimate arts. This book can open your awareness to the possibility of true, ecstatic loving and help you gather greater intimate wisdom for yourself to share in your intimate relationships.

Intimacy Tomes

Drawing from the knowledge of the sacred intimacy arts of ancient China, I thought it would be interesting to begin each part and skill set in this book with lore inspired by the Tao's second-century tales of the female immortal Su Nu Ching, who is legendary for introducing the intimacy arts in China.

The introductory stories told through the voice of Su Nu, who is often referred to as "the Immortal," combine aspects of my own learning and teaching experience of the Art of Love with selected aspects from the art's recorded mythic origins. The stories take place in a modern mystical setting where students are introduced to and guided through their apprenticeships of Intimate Wisdom skills, talents, and arts.

These stories are offered to your imaginative mind and inquiring heart as doorways to access new possibilities for you in love and intimacy.

The students could hear their teacher's voice being carried to them on the wind even before she arrived. The Immortal often utilized this teaching style to make sure that her students were present in the secluded Asian garden and prepared to tune in to the intimate lessons for the day. The students, who had been hand selected by the Immortal herself, were eager to discover more about the sacred love arts. Besides, their professor's out-of-this-world teaching style was thoroughly enjoyable. The students became ever more alert; they knew their teacher would be asking questions about what she had taught before she physically arrived. By the students' answers, she could assess their ability to perceive and trust what they could not see.

The teacher's voice was heard saying …

"Just as the Yellow Emperor of China, an inquisitive and willing pupil of the intimate arts, aptly learned from me the principles and skills to achieve exquisite love, sex, and intimacy, so will you.

"Today, you will begin to learn the personal skills of a Sacred Lover. This process can speed up and resolve the trial-and-error approach to intimacy that most of you have been taking, and it will help you let go of unneeded drama and frustration in your relationships."

For this lesson, Su Nu planned to privately instruct each student to cultivate the Sacred Lover within. This would develop the students' essential foundation for enjoying real intimacy as well as allowing them to master and share the Arts of Love.

"This is a crucial training period for each apprentice," continued the Immortal. "Your level of mastery in becoming a Sacred Lover will be reflected in the level of satisfying intimate relationships you will attract and the ease with which they will develop. The heights of pleasure and fulfillment of which you will be able to access in each area of intimacy, including lovemaking, will also be a result of your development as a Sacred Lover."

At that moment, the youthful, radiant—yet thousands of years old—Su Nu walked out of the waterfall and across the lawn to the front of the class. Looking around at her pupils, she was silently pleased, as she could see in their expressions that they were learning to perceive quickly.

"You will each be instructed in developing your personal skill set to create the love you want in your life. Each of you will begin this intimate journey with an introduction to the individual lessons and skills you need to enhance your openness and receptivity to love and pleasure. You will also learn powerful insights for choosing your sacred partner."

One by one she called each student to a private lesson in which she shared the secrets of becoming a Sacred Lover.

THE SACRED LOVER

PART ONE

Learn to Nurture and Develop the Lover Within
and Discover How to Invite Sacred Love into Your Life

Taking the First Step on the Journey to Love and Intimate Fulfillment

The quest for love and intimate fulfillment has taken place throughout history. It may be the greatest adventure ever undertaken.

While our human desire for love and connection is usually vibrant and alive in each of us, without a map, real intimacy can often be a struggle. Attracting the right partner and then enjoying and sustaining a fulfilling intimate life can seem like a dream just out of reach.

One of the greatest challenges that we face in creating what we want and need for ourselves in love and intimacy is a lack of knowledge and guidance. Cultural and community support, true role models, and wisdom have been virtually nonexistent in matters of love and intimacy. This is apparent in the high divorce rate, the millions of singles seeking relationships, and the percentage of couples who seem discontent. We all need more intimate wisdom.

Intimate wisdom is essential for a fulfilling intimate relationship. What we bring of ourselves to a relationship, who we choose as our partner, how we connect with our loved one, and how we demonstrate our love time and time again all define the quality of our relationship.

Despite the obstacles and perils of this quest for great love, there remains a burning flame of desire within us to have great love in our lives. Therefore, the journey continues to be worth taking. It's time for you to begin a new era in your journey of love and intimate fulfillment. This book is a map. All you have to do now is take the first step and discover who you are as a lover.

Do You Believe in Love?

If we desire love, we desire for it to be great! We desire a love relationship that makes us feel real passion and magic. We desire to be held deeply and loved romantically and ecstatically, while at the same time feel free to become more of who we dream of being. But do we actually believe that this kind of love exists?

Whatever You Believe is True

Whatever you believe in the fullness of yourself about love and experiencing love in your life becomes your truth and takes form in your reality. For great love to appear in your life, you have to first believe that it is possible.

Believing in great love requires imagining the possibility, then feeling the potential of great love inside of you. And lastly, it requires making choices to actualize the reality of great love in your life.

Once you believe in the possibility of great love, you have already started the process of creating the experience.

How Are You Showing Up for a Successful Relationship?

What we bring of ourselves to a relationship affects the kind of relationship that we attract and the kind of relationship that we will create. And to that end, I would like to ask you:

How are your attitude, emotions, energy, and behavior contributing to the success or disappointment of your relationships on an ongoing basis?

We are always creating a reality for ourselves in love based on how we show up for our relationships. How we show up for an intimate relationship is a product of our thoughts and beliefs, the lightness and heaviness in our hearts, and the openness and contraction within our physical bodies.

This mental, emotional, and physical—let's call it "wardrobe"—is what we consciously and unconsciously choose to show up with for intimate relationships, moment-to-moment and day-to-day, to create the success or disappointment that we are experiencing right now in love and intimacy.

Throughout Part One, we will discover how to make over our personal intimate wardrobe to help us show up ready for a successful relationship right now.

Only by understanding the roots of intimate wisdom can we truly access what it means to be a Sacred Lover. Let's get started with some of the love wisdom from China.

Skillful Lovers of China

China is legendary for its skillful lovers. A lover trained in the Art of Love is adept at showing up for a successful relationship by dissolving their resistance to intimacy and satisfying both their lover and themselves. A love master cultivates personal health, emotional well-being, and great artistry to experience and share tremendous passion, pleasure, and even ecstasy. At the same time, a love master can enrich the bond of intimacy in the relationship.

The powerful skills of these talented lovers developed from a deep understanding of and connectivity to nature. These love artisans recognized human intimacy to be a mere reflection of nature. By applying their observations of nature to love and sexuality, they developed mastery of the Art of Love.

The Art of Love is Rooted in the Philosophy of the Tao

This ancient Chinese tradition of skillful love and intimate pleasure was drawn out of the cosmology of Taoist philosophy. The ancient Taoists of China undertook the study of Tao and the principles of Yin—attributed to the feminine energy—and Yang—attributed to the masculine energy—as well as the cycles of nature as the foundation for having better health and relationships and a long life.

The following is a brief description of the philosophy of Tao. This ancient Eastern philosophy describes the beauty and sacredness of the intimate dance of oneness, duality, creation, and the return to wholeness, which is the ultimate experience of Sacred Love.

Oneness

In the beginning, there was oneness, a vast, dark, silent nothingness, the maternal, fertile womb of creation from which all life was born. This nameless source of all existence is Tao. Its nature is that of joy, peace, prosperity, and health. Oneness invisibly and silently composes, motivates, and compels the dynamic dance of all things.

Yin and Yang

One divided into two. Two became Yin and Yang. Yin and Yang revealed themselves as opposites: the moon and sun, earth and heaven, feminine and masculine.

Yin revealed her attributes as coolness, softness, wetness, receptivity, internalization, relaxation, darkness, and water. Yang demonstrated his attributes as heat, hardness, dryness, assertiveness, externalization, expansion, light, and fire.

These polar energies played, attracted, and magnetized each other into the dance of creation.

Creation

Yin and Yang seduced each other with their magnetic attributes, making love and creating infinite worlds, life forms, patterns, nature, humanity, and life experiences.

Yin and Yang's creative power is shared with all species. It flows through the natural world through seasons, elements, and sexual expression, assisting the plant and animal kingdoms as well as human beings in creating the continuation of life.

But human beings can also create in ways beyond the continuation of the species. Humans can utilize their creativity to build societies, produce artistic and social achievements, and create great love and bonding with one another.

All of creation eventually returns to oneness.

Reuniting with the One

In the beginning was the Tao. All things issue from it; all things return to it. To find the origin, trace back the manifestations. When you recognize the children and find the mother, you will be free of sorrow.

—Lao Tzu

As human beings, we long for a return to the *one*, that place of joy, bliss, play, peace, abundance, health, and love. Our longing is symbolized by our quest for Sacred Love, in finding true love, and becoming one with our divine counterpart.

Taoist sages—those individuals committed to traveling the way of Tao—became aware that intimate love was the projection of the soul's journey to transcend duality.

They realized that when intimate love supported the natural integrity of the individual, then health and happiness were enhanced. Health and happiness would also increase when intimate love supported the harmony within a relationship. On the other hand, when intimate love was expressed inappropriately, creating division and chaos, it took away health and happiness within the individual and his or her intimate relationship. The tradition of the Art of Love was developed with this understanding.

Creating Great Love

We can gain a great deal of wisdom from the ancient Chinese love masters. For achieving a great love experience today calls for two people who both desire and are capable of being love artisans—or what I call Sacred Lovers. These lovers bring passion, love, respect, and artistry to their experiences in an intimate relationship. This kind of skillful loving allows both individuals to be nurtured as a whole person, which in turn enriches their love life together.

What Makes Someone a Sacred Lover?

Sacred Lovers cultivate their capacity for Sacred Love.

Like a painter who develops certain skills, such as fine brushwork or painting with oils, Sacred Lovers develop their artistry for loving well. These love arts include self-respect and confidence, the courage to love, passion, great emotional and sexual expression, openness and receptivity, as well as a healthy commitment to the intimate relationship.

Sacred Lovers are generous in their capacity to give love, and they are available to receive the abundance of love their lover has to give. While an average lover is usually adept in a few areas of intimacy, rarely can they address another whole person. Average lovers often tend to stay close to the surface and perhaps dip a toe into real intimacy for brief periods of time. Sacred Lovers can more easily navigate the frightening waters and the opening to the ocean of ecstasy and bliss available in partnership. Sacred Lovers enjoy greater pleasure, deeper emotional union, and a mind-and-soul connection with their intimate partner.

Becoming a Sacred Lover

To acquire the artistry of a Sacred Lover, it is necessary to cultivate the lover within you. Enhancing your personal knowledge of love, nourishing your expertise in sharing love and intimacy, and increasing your discernment in identifying and attracting your Sacred Lover all prepare you for creating great love in your life.

As you move through this section of becoming initiated as a Sacred Lover, you will access greater insight and artistry within yourself to enjoy deeper satisfaction in an intimate relationship. The deepest desire of the Sacred Lover within you is to awaken and dance, blissfully and ecstatically, in the experiences of love, sex, and intimacy.

"Underneath every intimate relationship dynamic you have currently in your life, you are experiencing the effects of your own willingness and feelings of worthiness to love and be loved," began the Immortal to her first male student in a secluded area of the garden.

The Immortal then motioned for the young man to stand as a golden, full-length mirror instantly appeared in front of them. The Immortal continued. "Our thoughts, emotions, and bodies can allow in or deflect intimate experiences."

As she spoke these words, the usually invisible energy field of her pupil became clear to him in the mirror. It looked as if there was armor in front of his heart and parts of his body. The student, although accustomed to such magical happenings, looked with wonder, attempting to touch the armor he saw on his body. He realized that he could not feel the armor with his hands, but he sensed it was there.

The Immortal gave the student time to digest this visual experience and then continued. "Our formative intimate beliefs, past heartbreaks, and physical and emotional traumas can armor our hearts and bodies. They can affect the here and now by preventing us from fully allowing and enjoying the love that we desire.

"Where are you in relation to intimacy right now?" asked the Immortal. "Are you enthusiastic, energized, and open to the experience of intimacy? Or are you guarded, self-critical, and frustrated as you think of sharing yourself in love and sexual intimacy?"

The student reflected upon where he was within himself, then spoke. "There are a few things going on at once. I would say I feel enthusiasm, because I am ready for love to come into my life, and probably some fear as well."

"What is your fear?" asked the Immortal.

After a moment, the young man said, "I am scared of being heartbroken. If I really open up to someone … I feel that someone will not love me back the same way. And at the same time, I'm frustrated because I haven't experienced intimacy with someone in which we really connected and, you know, fit."

"Very good! You just articulated what your energy field is communicating outwardly and drawing to you."

The student, looking at himself in the mirror, then said with more than a hint of sarcasm and defeat, "Great."

The Immortal smiled to herself and said, "While you may be in a place right now that is not drawing to you what you really want in intimacy, you can change that."

"How?" asked the more hopeful student.

The Immortal explained. "By learning to open up to intimacy and love in the places you have closed yourself off from, you can dissolve your resistances and attract the love that fits you—in other words, a more passionate, satisfying, and nurturing intimate love."

The student's receptivity to the lesson became quickly apparent in the mirror as the appearance of his armor started to disappear. As his energy field became more translucent, a beautiful young woman appeared—seemingly from out of thin air—and gave him a kiss on the mouth. The young man blushed as the Immortal giggled with delight.

Skill 1: Opening Up to Intimacy and Love

We can learn how to open ourselves to profound intimacy—to experience rich love in our lives. The specific areas I will address in this chapter include: Removing Your Armor, Resistance, and Thresholds to Allow Love and Intimacy; Accepting Yourself and Inviting Great Love to Enter Your Life; Living Passionately; Honoring Yourself in Love; Boosting Your Vibe for Sacred Love; and Transforming Negative Emotions that Block Intimacy.

All of these sections work together to allow you to resolve negative emotional memories and intimacy patterns that inhibit the intimate connections you crave. They will enable you to regain confidence and open your mind to the possibility of Sacred Love. Skill One is the first skill you will need to develop to create the relationship you want. But it is also a skill that you will continue to cultivate throughout your development as a Sacred Lover.

Let's embark on exploring this essential Sacred Lover skill to enhance your connection to love and wholeness within yourself and bring forth your abundant loving nature.

Removing Your Armor, Resistance, and Thresholds to Allow Love and Intimacy

Intimate love and sexuality are exciting, intense, and fundamental aspects of our human experience. However, our ability to enjoy these experiences is always based on the intimate relationship we have with ourselves. What we think and feel and what we have encountered in experiences of both love and pleasure form our intimate makeup and influence the kinds of relationships we choose and co-create in our lives.

To be truly appreciated, tenderly touched, passionately kissed and made love to, emotionally supported, and meaningfully loved are intrinsic human desires for great intimacy. We crave these experiences because they lighten our hearts, ignite our bodies, and nurture our lives.

But why can it be so difficult to find and sustain these experiences?

Although we may deeply desire rich, intimate love, we may also have armor, resistance, and threshold points that keep us from claiming the treasures of a great relationship.

Sacred Love and sexual fulfillment take place proportionately to the openness in our bodies, hearts, minds, and spirits. The more closed off we are inside ourselves, the greater difficulty we have enjoying love and sex. The more openness we possess, the greater potential we have to experience satisfaction and bliss.

Our resistance to love and pleasure is based on what we learned from our primary caregivers and other significant relationship models. For example, if our parents did not demonstrate a lot of affection to each other, it may not be a natural, instinctive behavior for us to give affection to our lover. We may resist giving our lover the affection that they want from us, which causes them pain and frustration.

Our thresholds are defined by our cultural and personal belief systems. For example, we may believe that we have to look physically perfect or reach a certain level of success before we can find the love of our life. Consequently, we constantly criticize the way we look or our career progress. These criticisms create unintentional thresholds that hold us back from feeling great and at ease in the presence of someone who may be right for us.

Our armoring is built by our relationship disappointments and intimacy wounds. For example, if we have been sexually betrayed by a former lover, armoring can show up in the form of temporary sexual numbness or limited arousal. This armor can prevent us from opening up to a healthy intimate relationship with a trustworthy partner.

Intimacy can feel pleasing or terrifying to us, depending on whether we are currently experiencing resistance, thresholds, or armoring in a specific area. For instance, being asked to communicate our feelings may be enjoyable if we feel open to emotional intimacy or extremely painful if we have emotional resistance. And being physically naked next to our lover may be easy if we feel physically open to intimacy or terrifying if we have physical armoring.

Intimacy is our ability to share truth, genuineness, and closeness. Becoming intimate with ourselves may seem unusual, but it is a necessary step to building intimacy in our relationships. We can become intimate with ourselves by discovering more fully who we are and what truly brings us health and happiness. Personal intimacy involves self-reflection. Being active in developing a personal intimate relationship with ourselves helps us grow the roots for a more balanced emotional well-being. It can also help us access and heal the parts of us that have been weathered by intimate pain. A strong foundation of personal intimacy can give us guidance and help us trust our decisions.

As we enhance our personal intimate relationship with ourselves, we can more easily move through our intimate armor, resistance, and thresholds toward better relationships with others. We might move through the self-criticism threshold mentioned earlier by acknowledging that self-criticism is not going to bring us what we want and can, in fact, keep it away. This realization can transition us toward creating a supportive personal attitude that will enable us to let down our guard and attract the right relationship. We might move through the affection resistance mentioned earlier by addressing our core emotions about sharing affection. Our clarity on the subject will help us remove our armor so that we can begin to give and enjoy affection freely.

Moving through these thresholds dissolves our resistance to pleasure, love, and relationship intimacy. A confident, carefree relationship with the Sacred Lover within us attracts and develops healthier, more loving, and more fulfilling relationships.

The following sections and accompanying exercises will help you move through your particular armor, resistance, and thresholds in intimacy. Before continuing, you may want to take some time to write in your journal about your hopes and fears surrounding opening up to intimacy and love.

Accepting Yourself and Inviting Great Love to Enter Your Life

A great presence communicates confidence and manifests through inward relaxation, comfort in our own skin, and lightheartedness. Great presence can project physical sensuality, emotional centeredness, mental clarity, and inner radiance.

Presence exudes from our being without us having to utter a word. That said, words can also clarify and intensify our presence. Our presence is born of an acceptance of self and of our capacity to engage in and enjoy the present moment.

Many people believe that presence is something one either has or doesn't. While it is true that some people are born with great presence, it is essential to know that this trait can also be cultivated.

Self acceptance allows us to develop greater presence. It is a prerequisite to becoming a great lover and to attracting great love into our lives—for how accepting we are of ourselves is reflected in our relationships.

Most often, we accept only very specific parts of ourselves—the areas we like—and then we reject the others. Our rejection of parts of ourselves is usually in the form of self-criticism or subjecting ourselves to harmful "fix-me" regimes, such as dieting to extremes. Whatever we reject and resist in ourselves persists in our outer life. When we don't like ourselves, or even part of ourselves, we tend to attract partners who are inappropriate or who cannot meet our innermost needs. Self acceptance comes through learning to willingly embrace ourselves with appreciation.

Learning to accept our whole self is an important part of inviting great love into our life. Nurturing ourselves in healthy, substantial, and satisfying ways will help self-acceptance grow within us more easily and quickly.

Accepting Your Physical Body

Being fully accepting of our physical body in a society obsessed with physical perfection can be challenging. It is frustrating, even with the best of physiques, to feel as if we have to work endlessly to keep up our physical presence. However, it is important to learn to accept our bodies—including the aspects that we feel vulnerable about. For as we accept our bodies, we become much freer to express and experience love and our healthier, more sensual nature and sexuality.

Our bodies need to be nurtured in order to create greater acceptance.

Here are some ways to enhance acceptance of your physical body:

- Nurture your physical body with daily exercise that inspires you.
- Cook for yourself regularly throughout the week, being mindful of using healthy, great-tasting ingredients. Add your personal flair too—if you love beauty, you could prepare a salad with beautiful edible flowers, found in the produce section. If you are a nut lover, add roasted nuts.
- Get a massage or give yourself a massage with a sensual bath scrub.
- Instead of focusing on how you want your body to change, create fun ways to utilize and express your whole body more fully, like dancing wildly, gardening, or swimming.
- Send your body positive thoughts and words every day—for example, "Look how strong I am!" or "Wow, I look beautiful and vibrant today!"

Love Your Body Fully

Purpose:

When we love our bodies, we are more at ease with our physicality. Comfort with our bodies helps us to move gracefully and enjoy greater love and pleasure. Regardless of our size, shape, or seeming imperfections, we can regard our body with respect and without judgment. Our body is our personal universe pulsating with a unique soul, heart, and rhythm. When we acknowledge our body with love, we naturally treat it well and reap the benefits of a happier, healthier physical life. This technique helps to enhance a positive body image, release tension and physical stress, and increase physical vitality.

Practice:

- Visualize something that makes you feel like smiling, perhaps playing in a summer rain shower, a kiss, or a sunset on the beach.
- As you find this image, feel your mouth turn up into a sensuous smile.
- Feel the corners of your eyes turn up.
- Feel your face soften.
- Let your luscious smile melt away tension in your eyes, forehead, cheeks, ears, nose, lips, and skin.
- Feel your face melt into delightful relaxation.
- Now smile to your throat and neck.

- Feel your tightness dissolving.
- As your sensuous smile meets your shoulders, feel them evaporating into pure bliss.
- Smile to your heart; feel great love for your body in your heart.
- Feel this love coursing through your vital organs: first your lungs, then liver, kidneys, bladder, stomach, spleen, and pancreas.
- Sense the organs pulsating with energy, health, and vitality.
- Smile and allow joyous life to flow through your veins.
- Smile to your sexual organs.
- Indulge in your sense of pleasure.
- Smile and appreciate your divine arms, chest, belly, thighs, hips and legs.
- Let the smile flood your whole being with relaxation, vibrancy, and comfort.
- Feel your appreciation and self-love building.
- Feel the sacredness of your body.
- Keep this flow of positive feelings toward yourself throughout the rest of your daily activities.

Add this Love Your Body Fully practice to any exercise routine; it will enhance your positive mental and physical results.

Accepting your body more fully can bring up many emotions. For instance, it can make you aware of how you have judged yourself and picked apart your body and compared it to others' bodies. Recognize your feelings and know that your willingness to do this exercise, especially when those critical feelings come up, takes you closer to experiencing true physical acceptance. The more you do this, the easier it will be to feel great about your body. Others will notice and will follow your lead!

Accepting Your Emotions

We often believe that if someone finds out who we really are at the core—if they discover our insecurities and fears—or, indeed, if we fully express our passion and our fullest selves, we will not be loved. When we cannot express who we are emotionally or we express our emotions in a volatile way, this is a sign that we are in an unhealthy space with our emotions. But when we learn to accept our emotions, which arise as indicators of what is healthy or unhealthy for us, and communicate them when we need to, they no longer necessitate a negative, unhealthy charge. Commit to resolving and healing emotional pain from the past, which distorts the present, and accept growing into a healthier emotional you.

Our emotions need to be nurtured in order to create greater acceptance.

Here are some of the ways to accept your emotional self:

- Nurture your emotional well-being with private reflection. Journaling, meditation, and long walks provide great opportunities for reflection.
- Fill your mind with positive thoughts and inspiring words and images.
- Regularly share your feelings and thoughts with a trusted friend or partner.
- Surround yourself with upbeat, supportive friends and family who bring out the best in you.
- Take responsibility for your own emotions. Do not blame others for your emotional reactions to them.

Accepting Your Mind and Spirit

Acknowledge and accept your mind, the essence of your character, and your spirit, the invisible essence of who you are. Your mind defines your thoughts. Your spirit defines your most pervading inner and outer dispositions. Your mind can develop greater clarity and vibrancy in a state of acceptance. Your spirit can also develop greater peace in a state of acceptance. One way that we can embrace our mind is by making it our friend and not our critic during intimacy. A method of embracing our spirit is to invite the fullness of ourselves to share our experiences of love and sexuality. When we invite our mind into intimacy, we can enjoy each moment of sharing intimacy more fully. When we bring our spirit into intimacy, our resistance to rich, healthy, fulfilling love and sex melts away.

Our mind and spirit need to be nurtured in order to create greater self acceptance.

Here are some of the ways to enhance acceptance of your mind and spirit.

Mind:

- Choose to focus on the positive, and release dwelling on the negative.
- Transform your inner critic into a loving, empowering, supportive friend.
- Cherish yourself with loving actions and respectful deeds.

Spirit:

- Nurture your spiritual essence with a spiritual practice.
- Spend time in nature and around people who share your same value system.
- Make moment-to-moment choices that honor you, making you feel healthy and whole.

Living Passionately

Do you live a passionate life? Or do you spend much of your time watching, talking about, and envying how passionate and great other people's lives are?

Have you chosen a life path that brings out your best talents and is meaningful to you? Do you wake up enthusiastic about the day ahead?

Living passionately is, in essence, living from the heart. It is claiming and utilizing your gifts and talents in an avenue that is rewarding to you. It is about living a life that brings you the most joy and pursuing that life with commitment.

When we are not living a passionate life, we can have difficulty creating and sustaining a passionate, great relationship, because the principles for creating both are the same. Choosing a path or lover who is right for us and showing up for that experience moment-to-moment and day-to-day and then flowing with the cycles of building something wonderful are all vital steps that will bring forth a life and love life filled with passion.

Discovering and living our passion actually propels us to find and create a passionate, loving, intimate relationship, for once we are on the path of following our passion, we meet kindred spirits who are on the same journey.

Often, the most challenging obstacle to overcome is our own mind. When familiar or cultural messages play out in our heads—such as the idea that going for our passion isn't practical because it is hard or it won't happen, or the idea that we are not worthy enough or smart enough or young enough—then we have to slay those mental dragons in order for them not to defeat us before we even get started. We also have to continue to be diligent about clearing them from our minds when they appear again and again during our day-to-day journey.

As you create a passionate life, the excitement, high points, slow periods, seeming obstacles, and big payoffs will all help you more easily understand the process of creating an excellent relationship. Each process has these stages. Whatever success you are working toward—whether it be a great career or zeroing in on a great relationship—understand that stretching yourself and taking healthy risks are necessary to keeping passion alive and growing strong.

Think about the areas of your life that you are passionate about and have achieved success in. Write out the qualities you exhibited and the actions you took to reach your goals. Utilizing that same model, create a success strategy to achieve a passionate love life now.

Honoring Yourself in Love

If I love myself, I love you. If I love you, I love myself.
          —Rumi

How we are honoring ourselves becomes apparent in the words we use about ourselves, our behaviors, and the kind of relationships we create.

When we honor ourselves, we speak and act respectfully and lovingly toward ourselves, both when alone and around others. When we are honoring ourself in a love relationship, we feel good about ourselves, we feel recognized and supported by our lover, and we feel happy in our relationship.

If we are indiscriminate in our pursuit and choice of an intimate partner, we are not honoring ourselves. If we are having careless, reckless sex, we are not honoring ourselves. If we are betraying ourselves by being in a relationship with someone who does not recognize, love, or appreciate us, we are not honoring ourselves. And if we are accepting any form of abuse in an intimate relationship, we are not honoring ourselves.

Honoring ourselves in love is based on our self-worth. Our ability to love and appreciate ourselves and feel truly worthy of a great relationship results in our self-worth in the area of love. We can better honor ourselves by accepting ourselves, which we just addressed in Skill One, as well as by building integrity and trust in our own wisdom, which we will explore now.

Integrity

Our personal integrity is central to how we are and are not honoring ourselves.

Integrity can be described as the unity of the self. Our integrity is the strength of our individual core, which is made up of our physical, emotional, mental, and spiritual states. Being in integrity means not settling for less than what feels whole and harmonious to our entire selves.

Our sexuality, heart, mind, and spirit all have their own unique voices that speak inside of us. The sexual voice, the emotional voice, the mental voice, and the spiritual voice are made up of past conditioning, present experiences, and future hopes. Each of these voices may be communicating something different at the same time, which can cause us to be at odds internally about what we want from intimacy. This often keeps us from the intimate experiences that we most desire and need. For instance, our sexual voice may be saying, "I feel ashamed and don't deserve to enjoy myself," the heart voice may be saying, "I need love in my life that is equally returned," the mental voice may be saying, "I'm too old or insecure for the relationship I want," and the spiritual voice may be saying, "I want to have a divine relationship." We may not even realize that this conflict is taking place within us and preventing us from experiencing the love we want.

In the process of developing the Sacred Lover within us, we are moving toward nurturing a greater personal integrity. Instead of our sexual voice having its own agenda, the heart having another, and the mind and the spirit also wanting something different, these separate voices begin to harmonize their desires and act together in unison.

When we achieve this level of integrity, we experience harmony within ourselves and create it in our relationships. Our mind and our body communicate health. Our heart loves easily and feels happiness. Our spirit, the fullness of who we are, is invited into our life experiences.

Integrating the sum of all parts of oneself is a tall task. However, integrity can be accomplished by continuing to nurture our self acceptance emotionally, physically, mentally, and spiritually. We gain greater clarity and confidence in what is truly nurturing and healthy for us the more we do it.

Through this process of integration, it becomes easier to experience a sense of alignment, honesty, and wholeness within the self, which is the central development of the Sacred Lover.

It is this unified clarity—our integrity—that develops in us better discernment, meaning we make decisions based on considering our whole selves. As we take more actions that nurture the integrity of our whole selves, we will also feel more truly rewarded.

Integrity always gives us the ability to take responsibility for our own intimate experience and to say yes or no with confidence when we make intimate decisions, thus helping us to create a healthy and fulfilling intimate relationship.

Building Integrity

Purpose:
Building your integrity daily enriches personal and relationship fulfillment.

Practice:
- Strengthen your individual core, which is made up of your physical, emotional, mental and spiritual states, by developing your self acceptance in these areas.
- "It is not about him or her." Deal with the reasons you sabotage yourself from finding and experiencing a great relationship. Perhaps write these reasons in your journal.

- Honor yourself in your intimate interactions by respecting your physical body, emotional well-being, mind, and spirit—and in return, accept from others *only* respect for all these areas of yourself.

- Ask yourself: do I respect (love, value, nourish, support) myself? Answer yes or no to the following:

  Do I respect my physical body?

  Do I respect my sexuality?

  Do I respect my emotions?

  Do I respect my intellect?

  Do I respect my career/life path?

  Do I respect my spiritual path?

- In addition, ask yourself: how am I integrated right now?

  Do I feel integrity within my heart, body, mind, and spirit?

  What areas feel the most integrated? What areas feel the least integrated?

  Is my ability to connect to someone special increasing?

  Is my ability to form a more honest intimate exchange increasing?

  Do I desire an entirely satisfying experience of love, sex, and intimacy?

- Act respectfully and with integrity toward your partner physically, emotionally, mentally, and spiritually.

Lies and Manipulation

Lies and manipulation are based on our feelings of low self-esteem, a lack of integrity, and powerlessness.

Lies are a great indication of where we do not feel good enough, or strong enough, to share our true self and be honest.

We engage in manipulation when we do not feel confident that we can have what we need and are too weak to ask for it or take action toward it in a healthy way. Manipulators play games and seek out another person's vulnerability to get what they want.

Lies and manipulation are not only a betrayal of others, but a betrayal of ourselves; they affect our integrity. When we are not honest with ourselves about what our real needs are and do not communicate them truthfully, those needs live in the shadows of our psyche, causing us to act out in unconscious ways.

Stepping away from a pattern of lies and manipulation requires coming more fully into a state of integrity within ourselves and claiming the courage to be honest with ourselves. We can strengthen our personal integrity by developing healthy communication skills and taking positive action toward what we need. If a temptation to lie surfaces, don't be afraid to analyze why. Speak with a trusted friend, your partner, or a therapist about your struggle. By confronting honestly and clearly what is behind your feelings to lie and manipulate, you will find yourself on the edge of a new personal integrity and a healthier, more passionate relationship with love.

Choosing Honesty Over Lies

Purpose:
Asking and answering questions about the feelings behind your lies and manipulation can strengthen your awareness of the vulnerable areas you need to address in order to promote self-esteem and greater integrity. This practice can be a walking, thinking meditation, or you can write about it in your journal.

Practice:
Ask yourself:
- Do I deny parts of myself that are mandatory to my well-being? If yes, how?
- Do I experience emotional, sexual, mental, and spiritual fulfillment? If yes, how? If no, how could I change that?
- Can I share stress and responsibilities with a loved one? If no, how could I begin to?
- Do I feel depleted in an area of my relationship? If yes, where?
- Do I feel cherished and loved? If yes, by whom? If no, how can I change that?
- Do I feel insecure? In what ways? How can I change that?

Notice how your answers address the areas where you feel most vulnerable and which may, in turn, cause you to lie and manipulate. By answering the questions above, you can strengthen the areas in you that will enhance your self-esteem, honesty, and integrity.

Honoring yourself and developing your integrity in love can be a super-challenging process at first. If you enjoy a challenge, then these are very exciting, productive processes for you to get started on. If you tend toward wanting to avoid a challenge, the great news is that honoring yourself and developing your integrity will become less and less difficult for you in a short period of time. These processes will also become more fun and feel incredibly empowering the more you cultivate them. And the rewarding results are that your obstacles in intimacy will begin to vanish.

The teacher was reclining along the sensually draped daybed in the garden. Her students relaxed on lush pillows, waiting for the next lesson to begin. The teacher always appeared at leisure. She exuded a natural openness, relaxation, and lightheartedness that made it very inviting for her students to be in her presence. At times the teacher would not teach with words, but just sit with her students, silently enjoying a connection with them.

This lesson would be different. She had gathered all of her students in the garden to participate. There would be communication, but not a kind that her students had experienced before.

One wind chime began softly ringing, then another, and then another, until the garden was filled with the sounds of different musical chimes. Some harmonized with one another, and others had their own pitch that sounded dull, muted, or shrill. Some seemed close and loud; others sounded faint and distant. The students all thought that the Immortal was ringing the chimes, but they did not see the chimes moving.

After several minutes, the Immortal spoke with a gentle smile. "The sounds that you are hearing are coming from within you. They are happening inside of you." Immediately, the students were perplexed.

"The sound that you hear the loudest is your own tone of vibration."

Some of the more advanced students seemed pleased with this news. More of the newer students seemed to recoil in embarrassment. This was normal, as the newer students were still unaware of their ability to develop the quality of their personal vibrational tone to attract and experience fulfilling love.

The Immortal continued. "Your vibration is the condition of the lightness of your energy that proceeds from your mind, heart, and body. Your vibration can be refined. Sacred Lovers refine their vibration until they reach natural harmony and radiate lightness both inwardly and outwardly."

A male student asked, "How does my vibration affect me as a Sacred Lover?"

"The more positive and loving your vibration is, the greater your ability to experience the best sensations of love. Loving vibrations attract a magnetic flow of love more fully into your life.

"You can raise your vibration at any time to attract a matching partner or achieve a deeper level of mental, emotional, and sexual harmony in your relationship. Are you ready to learn how?" she asked.

The class replied with affirmative eagerness.

Boosting Your Vibe for Sacred Love

During the first encounter with a potential partner, the only thing we want to know is whether we will vibe together. And we instantly know if we do or not. We will walk away thinking, I love this person's vibe, I don't like this person's vibe, or I'm not sure about this person's vibe.

Why?

We may or may not be aware of it, but we are really tuning in to see if our physical chemistry, our thoughts, and so on are on the same frequency as this person.

Our vibe is actually our vibration, our current of energy that we exude from within ourselves to others. When we meet a matching vibration, we feel excitement, harmony, relaxation, and happiness. When we meet a mismatched one, we feel exhausted, bored, irritated, and confused. We also may meet a middle-of-the-road match that tilts slightly to one side or the other, causing us to feel both some excitement and some confusion. These are the connections that tend to take longer to figure out.

We are always creating a reality for ourselves based on the energy frequency we emit. Our vibration can be consistent or can fluctuate, depending on our thoughts, our emotional mood, the state of our health, the food we have eaten, and the exercise we have done. Our field of experiences in an intimate relationship proceeds from our consistent or fluctuating vibrations and the responses to these vibrations from our partner or potential partner.

If you are seeking a sacred relationship or want to enhance the one you already have, one of the quickest and most effective skills you can learn is how to boost your vibration. What you are about to discover is how to raise your personal vibration to the right frequency to have the love you want in your life. To boost your overall vibration, we will address your mental, emotional, and physical vibe.

How Open and Positive is Your Mind?

Mental Vibe

As I stated at the beginning of Part One: The Sacred Lover, our beliefs are fundamental to having great love in our lives. In this section, let's take a deeper look at our beliefs to see how they are creating our current vibration for sharing an intimate relationship.

What have you imagined for yourself in love? What do you believe about love? Do your beliefs and imagination match your experience of love today? If not, why not?

Imagine for a minute or two what you want to experience in love. You may even want to write down what you are imagining. Can you envision for yourself an emotionally nurturing, generous, and fulfilling relationship? A sexier, more passionate relationship? A mentally and spiritually stimulating and inspiring relationship? A heart, body, and soul Sacred Love relationship? Now close your eyes and visualize it.

Once you have opened your mind to a bigger vision of love, your energy vibration rises, and your receptivity to those experiences increases.

To keep our energy moving in an increasingly positive vibration, we have to address our underlying beliefs about love. We can get stuck in our negative thoughts: "My partner will never give me the love and intimacy I desire," "I'm not good enough for the relationship I want or have," "I'm not in the right town or at the right place in my life for the right relationship," "All relationships are difficult," or "There are no good men or women out there."

What kind of vibration would these ideas emit from you? You have probably guessed the answer: negative vibrations.

Let's change these thoughts to ones that will create the vibrations that will give you what you really want.

Examining Your Beliefs

Purpose:
Examining your beliefs about love can help you discover why you attract certain experiences, both positive and negative, in love and intimacy.

Practice:
Right now I would like you to take an exam. Take out your journal and examine your beliefs about love.

Write down the most positive belief that you have about love. Skip down the page, leaving some space. Now name the most self-defeating belief you have about love.

Our beliefs about love are reinforced all around us. How are your beliefs being reinforced in your life right now? In the first section, write down how your positive beliefs about love are being reinforced in your life.

Now, in the second section, write down how your negative beliefs about love are being reinforced. Notice which belief has more reinforcements in your life.

When love is not adding up to what you want, then more of your focus is on your negative belief system. This negative viewpoint creates a negative vibrational field for you in love, which can bring you great frustration, disappointment, and discouragement.

The more positive your thoughts, the more positive the field of experiences that you are creating. As you increase your positive thoughts and beliefs, you will begin to change your vibrational field for the better and see more love and loving people coming into your life. More potential partners and loving experiences in your relationships will magically begin to appear.

Your challenge is to begin to sharpen your focus on your best beliefs about love and look for signs that reinforce them. Think of couples you know who are creating a great relationship. Read inspiring love poetry out loud. Tear out photos from magazines that inspire you to great love and make a vision board to put up on your wall or inside your closet door. Watch movies about great love. Notice a passing conversation of people expressing love to each other. Take note of the ways that people are demonstrating their love to you every day with a compliment, a call, a hug, a gift, a loving gesture, or an intimate experience.

As you increase your positive vision of love, you have to choose better ideas and beliefs to think, say, and hold dear. Doing so will help you move toward what you really want for yourself in love: a truly satisfying relationship.

How Light is Your Heart?

Emotional Vibe

A fascinating scene depicted in ancient Egyptian art is "The Weighing of the Heart." In the Egyptian Book of the Dead, a deceased Egyptian stands at his judgment before a huge scale. On one side of the scale is his heart placed in a jar. On the other side of the scale is a feather. All those around him wait to see if his heart is light enough for him to enter heaven.

If you were to be judged right now, would your heart gain entrance into heaven? Would your heart be light as a feather? Heaven and great love are synonymous. We use the term "I'm in heaven" when our heart is light—meaning when we are happy and having a wonderful time, as well as when we fall in love.

The relationship between a light heart and the love we want is apparent in the attractive appeal of a sense of humor. I hear from women over and over that one of the qualities they find most appealing in a man is a sense of humor. And the same holds true for many men. We love someone who will make us laugh, who can help us forget about our tough days and life challenges and just have a good time.

A consistently heavy heart, which either shuts us down or brings out volatile emotions, is a turn-off. It puts a halt to moving into more intimate territory with someone we love. What causes heaviness and volatility are unresolved emotions that block us from enjoying life and experiencing the intimacy we want. Past heartbreaks and physical/emotional traumas can prevent us from having an open and light heart and from fully enjoying the love that we desire. Although we long to experience love—even great love—we may be sending out the opposite signal time and time again with a heavy heart vibration.

Our emotional frequency objective is to remove these barriers from our heart by releasing old emotions like pain and regret. If we have had a heavy heart for an extended period of time, it is important to seek the help of a therapist or counselor to address our emotional pain. But generally, we ourselves can restore emotional lightness with laughing, being positive, practicing meditation regularly, and forgiving ourselves and others.

This would be a good time to write out what can make your heart heavy and some of the ways you can lighten your heart now. You can also use the practices throughout Part One, such as Building Integrity, Letting Go of Your Ghost Stories Around Intimacy, and Emotional Alchemy to support you in transforming a heavy heart into one "as light as a feather."

By developing a light heart you raise your emotional vibration. Your light heart can support you in having more fun, joy, and creativity in developing a passionate, loving intimate relationship.

How Energized and Receptive is Your Body?

Physical Vibe

Lastly, we are going to address the physical energy vibration that we show up with for love. Our bodies carry an energy that is made up of what we put into our body, what exercises we do, how quickly and easily we release stagnant energy, and how we exchange energy with others.

We can clear out our old, toxic physical energy by eating cleansing foods like fresh fruits and vegetables. We can also nourish what the ancient Taoists refer to as "chi," or vital energy, in our bodies through daily physical exercise and other chi-enhancing practices such as, Qigong, Yoga, hiking, and dancing. Our physical energy plays a large part in our love frequency. Our physical energy frequency attracts our partners to us and brings forth our experiences in love and intimacy.

The art of ecstatic and sacred sexuality is about energy exchange. This is one of the great teachings that the ancient Chinese love masters imparted. The more awakened we are to our own energy, the clearer our energy becomes. The greater our ability to move energy through our body and our partner's body, the more ecstatic, healing, and empowering our sexuality will be.

Thus, our objective for love and intimacy is to raise our body's energy level to a clearer, higher frequency so that we can have more fulfilling intimacy and sexuality.

Love Vibrations Exercise

Note: This is an exercise from *Fit for Love*, which is a mindful movement practice that I developed in the process of working with many clients and students over the years. Its purpose is to support the students' intimate journey of moving out of their heads and into their hearts and bodies in order to experience real intimacy. Drawing from the principles and exercises of Tai Chi, Qigong, Yoga, and Kung Fu, this movement practice can profoundly boost your physical vibration, which in turn will improve your love life. You will find several other exercises like this throughout the book.

Purpose:

Vibration is the sensation of energy flow. By activating the energy flow of love in our bodies, we can let go of our bodies' resistances and experience the greatest sensations of love. Love Vibrations attract the flow of love more fully into our lives.

Practice:

- Begin in standing position. Stand with your feet hip-width apart, and bend the knees slightly.
- Smile. Begin to shake. Feel your body loosen and become free as you shake.
- Breathe in and make the sound "hawww." This is the heart sound, which awakens the love energy and sends vibrations of love through the body. Feel the shaking relaxing the body and eliminating stress and tension. (We will go into the use of this sound in more depth in the section of Emotional Alchemy.)
- Circle the pelvis as you shake. First circle in one direction and then in the other direction. Feel yourself opening up energy in the pelvis.
- Stir the love vibrations into the pelvis by making the "hawww" sound and focusing your attention on the pelvis. Smile and breathe.
- Bring the arms up. Shake faster. Smile, breathe, and continue to make the "hawww" sound.
- Bring the arms down, and shake faster. Send the sound "hawww" down through the pelvis and the legs. Then send the sound up the body toward the crown of your head as you move the arms upward.
- Repeat three to six times.
- Start to slow down.

Notice the pleasant vibrations in your body. The body is vibrating with heart energy. This exercise opens and awakens your physical energy for love.

Transforming Negative Emotions That Block Intimacy

Our ability to create a successful relationship has a lot to do with our emotions, which we can address in various ways, including through mental, spiritual, and physical avenues. Let's explore our emotions and how we can transform them to create the love that we want.

Confronting Our Ghosts of Intimacy

When we hold onto our fears and old negative emotions concerning relationships, it is challenging to be fully present for intimacy. We seek diversions to prevent ourselves from being really open and available for love. Work, television, children, housework, and exhaustion are some of these prime examples that can keep us from finding a great relationship or strengthening our current relationship. The following practices will aid you in letting go of your relationship fears and negative emotions, allowing you to claim the rich rewards of great love and intimacy.

Letting Go of Your Ghost Stories About Intimacy
Mental and Spiritual Practices to Transform Negative Emotions that Block Intimacy

We all have different make-ups that draw us to specific practices and activities at different times. The following practices offer several possible ways you can confront and clear your own ghost stories and intimate emotions in the way most appropriate for you. As you progress through the rest of this book, and as you practice the exercises detailed here, you will develop an intuitive feel for the methods that benefit you most. Choose the exercises that most resonate with you.

Getting Your Ghost Stories Out of Your Head
Most of us have a ghost story that holds us back from experiencing the love that we desire. Take out your journal and write out your ghost story, or stories, that still haunt your experience of love and sexual fulfillment today. Take about twenty minutes, or as long as you need, to do this exercise. Read your words aloud and acknowledge the feelings that surface about your ghost story.

Making Your Ghost Stories Disappear
To make our ghost stories disappear, we first have to give ourselves permission to let go. Often, we don't realize that we are holding on to our stories, because they provide us a false sense of

safety. That's why we can get into a pattern of hashing them out over and over again and resisting letting them go.

Now, close your eyes and ask yourself: am I ready to let go of this story?

Your mind may immediately say yes, but move your awareness down to your heart and ask your heart the same question, then do the same with your body. If you feel resistance in any area, ask that part of yourself, "What do you need from me to let go?" If the answer is, for instance, "I need you to forgive yourself," then do that. If the answer includes seeking something from someone else—such as an apology, love, or physical comforting—there is no guarantee that will be possible. Instead, give these things to yourself. Apologize to your heart, comfort your body with a bath or a massage, and be loving toward yourself. Once your whole self has given you permission to let go, it is much easier for your ghosts to move on. Make them vanish by transforming them into empowering love lessons.

Finding the Love Lessons in Your Ghost Stories to Enhance Intimacy

Now that you have explored your ghost stories and given yourself permission to let go, you are ready to cast your intimate history in a positive light. In your journal, I want you to write out how this intimate history has shaped you for the better. Take fifteen minutes to do this exercise, or as long as you need.

Here are some questions you should ask yourself:

- What are the love lessons and skills that my ghost stories have given me?
- Have they given me better discernment?
- Have they helped me develop healthier boundaries?
- Have they made me choose a partner more carefully?
- Have they helped me discover another person's blind spots or challenge areas more quickly?
- Have they helped me avoid a disaster?
- Has my history given me better emotional skills to communicate my truth in a loving way?
- Has my intimate history given me the courage to become more loving toward myself and others?
- How has my intimate history prepared me to create and share the love I desire?

Look at your old ghost story and the new story you have just written. Your story is the way you choose to see it. It is time to move past your fears with a new courage to love.

Fire Ritual
Rituals have been utilized by every culture throughout human history to honor and support change and celebrate the moment. The following fire ritual is designed to help you let go of the ghost story or stories that have held you back from intimacy.

In many ways fire is the perfect symbol for this ritual because it is a literal and figurative representation of burning our old stories into ashes. When we do this, we purify our heart and mind. At the same time, we are able to ignite the flame inside us and open ourselves up to even greater new experiences of intimacy and love.

Light a fire. It can be a candle, a fire in a fireplace, or a fire pit in your backyard.

Make an intention to release your old intimate ghost stories. Place the paper that you wrote your old stories on in the fire and let it burn. Allow this ritual to signify the letting go of your ghost stories that are holding you back from intimacy.

Now take your rewritten intimate history and place it next to your heart. See it as the gift and opportunity that your experiences in intimacy have brought you. If possible, walk in a circle around the fire. If it is not possible, walk in a circle in front of the fire. (This circle signifies your "Love Wheel of Fortune" turning again.)

Bring the gifts from this ritual into a new, fulfilling experience of intimacy. You may choose to honor your rewritten story by keeping it in a special box. You can place this box in your bedroom to inspire positive energy in your love life, or you can choose to discard the story by burning it in the fire as well.

Letting go of your ghost stories by transforming them and then releasing them in a fire ritual can be a very emotional process. You might want to go for a walk, exercise, do something fun, or even celebrate in some way afterwards.

Emotional Alchemy

Removing our emotional armoring may require deeper support before we can fully release our capacity to invite fulfilling love and intimacy into our lives. Long-held emotions and subsequent reactions that have inhibited intimate connection may require us to take a deeper look into our hearts and bodies.

We can carry our emotions about intimacy not only in our mental thoughts but also in our hearts and bodies. The openness in our hearts and the ease in our physical bodies reflect the emotional memories and patterns that we have held over time. Our level of emotional and physical openness shows up in how we express ourselves intimately. The following practice is designed to alchemize deep intimate emotions and enable us to express and receive emotional intimacy.

First I will explain the emotional centers that are central to working with this Emotional Alchemy practice.

Emotional Centers

The understanding of the mind-body relationship is one of the fundamental arts that the ancient Chinese love masters studied to enhance their skill for achieving health, vitality, and the ability to love well. What they discovered was that our emotions originate and tend to be stored in specific areas of our body. These specific areas are called energy centers. When we have an abundance of specific positive emotions attributed to a specific energy center, that area of our body is more open, and energy flows from and to it in a healthy way. The area of our life connected to this energy center feels good and functions optimally.

For instance, if we feel an abundance of love in our hearts, our hearts are healthier and more open. We attract and enjoy more love in our lives. When we have an abundance of specific negative emotions attributed to a specific energy center, that area of our body is more closed off. Energy has a difficult time flowing from or to it, and we may even feel pain or very little sensation in this area of our body. As a result, the part of our life that is connected to that specific energy center functions less efficiently. For example, if we have felt emotionally heartbroken by a person in our life and have not fully resolved and let go of that story, we tend to not open up our hearts as easily to new intimate experiences and may have trouble expressing love in a healthy way. In turn, it becomes difficult to experience satisfying emotional relationships.

We will explore energy centers and the movement of energy throughout this book for the purpose of enhancing our experience of love and intimacy. There are many energy centers, such as the third eye (psychic) center, located at the mid-eyebrow, and the spiritual center, located at the crown of the head—which you will learn about later in Part Two: The Talent of Loving Another. However, in this practice of Emotional Alchemy, we will focus specifically on our exploration of the two primary energy centers that relate to love and intimacy: the Heart and the Sexual Palace.

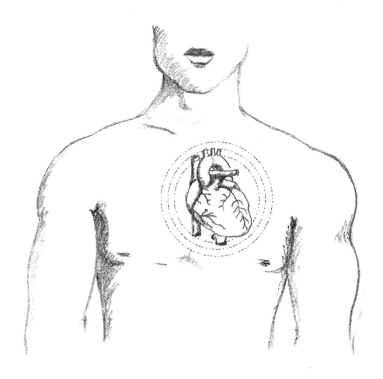

HEART CENTER

The Heart is located in the middle left side of the chest, and for the purposes of this practice, this is the Heart's energy center. (In other practices, you may be asked to focus on the Heart Center by bringing your attention to the area between the breasts.) This center encompasses the physical Heart and controls the circulation of blood through the veins and arteries. It is also the emotional center of love, joy, and self acceptance. Connecting mindfully with our Heart Center can increase our passion and our loving feelings.

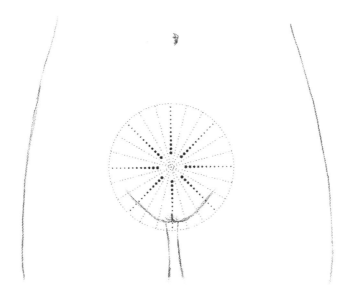

SEXUAL PALACE

Taoists refer to our sexual region as the Sexual Palace. A palace is a place of beauty, lavish splendor, and sensuous pleasure. Our sexual center is the sacred home of pleasure and joyous experiences within our bodies. Acknowledging our sexuality as a sacred palace can help us regain a healthy sexual connection and enhance sensual feelings of pleasure.

For women, the Sexual Palace area begins at the midpoint between the ovaries and includes the internal sexual organs, such as the ovaries and the uterus, as well as the external female genitalia. For men, this area begins at the pubic bone and contains both the external male genitalia, such as the penis and scrotum, and the internal prostate gland.

Choose the emotional center that is most appropriate for you to reflect on at this time. Focus on the Heart or the Sexual Palace to resolve the emotions that are blocking the flow of intimacy in your life. Later, when you have deepened your ability to sink into the method, you can add both the Heart and Sexual Palace into one alchemy practice.

This exercise will enhance your positive emotions toward intimacy that will in turn support a healthy, sexy and loving relationship. By taking your time to reflect and transform the emotions in each emotional center you will build confidence in your ability to move through your emotional intimacy thresholds to experience the intimacy that you desire. The same preparation is utilized for both practices. Each practice begins with an emotional purpose. Instructions follow afterward. I will start by guiding you through the alchemy to Open Your Heart.

Emotional Alchemy

Deep Emotional Practices That Transform Negative Emotions That Block Intimacy

Preparation:

- Find a quiet place to meditate.
- Sit with a straight back either on the edge of a chair or cross-legged on the ground.
- Touch the upper palate of your mouth with your tongue.
- Rest your hands palm-side down on your knees.
- Smile inwardly.
- Feel your mind and body relaxing.

Open Your Heart

Purpose:

Open your Heart to intimacy. Clear away insecurities and heartache. Access greater passion and love.

Awareness Instruction:

- Close your eyes.
- Feel your smile flowing to your Heart. (Location: in the middle left side of your chest.)
- Observe the Heart.
- Be aware of how your Heart feels.
- Notice if you have feelings of impatience, insecurity, inadequacy, hurt, or heartache.

You may feel impatient about finding the right partner, insecure about being lovable, or inadequate about your skill as a lover. You may feel emotionally hurt or have an old heartache that hasn't gone away. Take a moment to be present with your emotions. As you bring your awareness to them, feel the emotions begin to dissolve as you give your loving attention to them.

Clearing Your Heart Emotions Practice:

- Breathe into the Heart and exhale the Heart sound quietly: "haawww." This sound can resolve an old heartache or release very immediate feelings of insecurity. This practice can also boost openness, self-love, and the ability to more easily express love to another.
- Release the deeper emotions of impatience, insecurity, inadequacy, hurt, or heartache from your Heart and mind through the sound.
- Breathe naturally for thirty to sixty seconds while smiling into your Heart. Feel the Heart deeply relax.
- Repeat three to nine times.
- Experience for several minutes your Heart growing lighter. Feel the positive emotions of self-love as well as passion and love for others building in your Heart.

Be aware of any feelings that have arisen and been cleared in this Heart-Opening alchemy process. Note for yourself what you feel right after the exercise and then throughout the day. From just ten minutes of practice, you can continue clearing emotions even hours later.

Clear Your Sexual Palace Emotions

Begin with the Emotional Alchemy preparation instructions.

Purpose:

This practice will help you attune with your Sexual Palace. Clear away shame, fear, hurt, and betrayal. Enhance your experience of pleasure.

Awareness:

- Close your eyes.
- Feel your smile flowing into your Sexual Palace. (Location: mid and lower pelvic region.)
- Observe your Sexual Palace and be aware of any negative emotions there, such as guilt, shame, fear, hurt, or betrayal. Perhaps you carry shame for expressing your sexual self or guilt for experiencing pleasure, or perhaps you judge yourself for a past sexual experience. You may also feel hurt from or fear of a sexual betrayal.
- Remain objective and compassionate toward yourself as you become aware of these emotions.

Clearing Your Sexual Palace Emotions Practice:

- Breathe into your Sexual Palace area.

- Exhale the Sexual Palace sound quietly: "heee."

- Feel the sound releasing the negative emotions of shame, guilt, fear, hurt, or betrayal from your Sexual Palace.

- Repeat three to nine times.

- Rest and breathe naturally into your Sexual Palace. Observe what is taking place there.

- Now smile and connect to the positive feelings of pleasure and creativity in the Sexual Palace. Do this for several minutes.

Be gentle with yourself as you clear your Sexual Palace emotions. Long-buried emotions may surface even hours later. Hug yourself, love yourself, and, at your own pace, continue to create inner sexual harmony with the help of this alchemical sound.

Fit For Love

Many people gravitate to physical movement to help them process emotions. These *Fit for Love* exercises are designed specifically to help you easily dissolve your emotional and physical resistance to intimacy in order to enjoy greater sexual pleasure and receive more emotional love. You can practice them on your own or with a partner.

Fit for Love
Physical Practices to Transform Negative Emotions That Block Intimacy

Sensual Body Flow Exercise

Purpose:
Sensuality is a natural attribute that can make us feel more harmoniously connected to our bodies. This movement allows us to awaken and nurture our sensual, sexual body essence with love.

Practice:
- Begin in standing position with the feet pointed straight ahead, hip-width apart, and arms down at your side.

- Bend into the knees slightly, and make a figure-eight with the hips.
- Practice the figure eight several times prior to beginning the full movement.
- Once you are comfortable with the figure-eight movement, inhale and turn your waist to the left.
- Lift the right arm up from your side and across in front of your body at a sixty-degree angle.
- Then continue to move the arm straight upwards over the head.
- Exhale.
- Simultaneously, make the figure eight with the hips as you slowly guide the hand down the center of your body, grazing your face, throat, chest, and torso.
- Repeat with the left arm.
- Inhale and turn the waist to the right.
- Lift the left arm up and across the front of your body at a sixty-degree angle and then upwards over the head.
- Exhale.
- Begin the figure eight with the hips.

Now,

- Draw the heavenly energy down through your sensual body as you slowly move your hand downward.
- Feel the sensuousness of your hand grazing your face, throat, chest, and torso.
- Feel love from nature nurturing your sensuality.
- Sink into the sensuousness of the movement.
- Repeat five to ten times.

Opening to Infinite Love Exercise

***Purpose*:**
Infinite love is available to us in every moment. We just have to remember to open up to it. In this movement, we take a moment to open and receive the infinite love of nature and the universe.

Practice:

- Start in standing position with the feet pointing straight ahead, hip-width apart.
- Bring the hands palm-side up beside the hips.
- Then circle the hands backward so that the fingertips are pointing behind you.
- Now circle your hands and arms forward, and cross the elbows in front of the heart.
- Tuck the buttocks in and slightly arch the back.
- Open your arms to the infinite universe.
- Open to infinite love; breathe it in.
- Take three to six deep breaths.

Now,

- Slowly come back to a straight, standing position.
- Bring the feet together.
- Using your hands, draw the energy down to your navel.
- Circle the energy under the navel.
- Digest the love and breathe easily.

Sexy Serpent Exercise

Purpose:

The serpent is a sexy, powerful creature. Throughout history in many of the world's ancient and contemporary traditions, the serpent has symbolized healing, transformation, and enlightenment. This movement allows us the opportunity to tap into our sexy nature and transform our bodies for physical love.

Practice:

- From standing position bring your legs together and place your hands in a "V" position in front of the Sexual Palace. The fingertips of both hands point downwards, touching one another, while the palms remain open. Take a moment to recognize that your sexuality is sacred.
- Bend your knees and begin to move your hips to one side while your arms—with the hands still in prayer position—move to the other side. Continue to move your hips back and forth at the same level while your arms and hands "snake" upwards toward the sky.

- Once the arms are above the head, draw in the heavenly energy by breathing in.
- Bring your hands down the same way you brought them up, as you begin to "snake down." The hips move to one side, while the arms move to the other side as you snake down toward the earth.
- See if you can snake down close to the earth, then come back up to a standing position with the legs and feet together.
- Place the hands in a prayer position in front of the sexual center. Breathe in and out of the Sexual Palace. Smile.

As you discovered in Opening Up to Intimacy and Love, welcoming real intimacy into your life follows naturally when you make ongoing progress in accepting and honoring yourself, living passionately, building integrity, and transforming your negative emotions.

The Immortal asked her student if she would like a drink. As it was getting warm out, the student nodded in appreciation. Su Nu—with her golden boa constrictor laced around her shoulders—offered the student a refreshing elixir to help create the atmosphere for the lesson she was about to undertake. The student carefully took the tonic and proceeded to drink. While she sipped the secret recipe, the teacher commenced.

"Sexuality is the source of great creative power. Sexual energy can create or diminish life itself. A love artisan understands that their awareness and use of sex can either offer temporary benefits or a sacred tonic for regeneration and lasting intimate fulfillment. Sex as a sacred experience extends and enriches pleasure and bonding. Sex expressed sacredly can also open up the door to perceive the secrets of the universe. A love artist chooses to cultivate their sexuality as a sacred art."

A gentle wind blew through the flowering tree of white and fuchsia blossoms that stood beside Su Nu and her student, stirring up the sweet aroma of its flowers. The Immortal stopped and closed her eyes to drink in its sensational perfume. The boa followed suit. Su Nu opened her eyes and said, "Take a breath of this intoxicating pleasure." Her pupil joined in.

The wise master said, "True pleasure leads you to who you really are, the essence of yourself that is bliss and boundless joy. Pleasure enlivens our bodies, inspires our steps, and melts away our burdens.

"Your relationship to pleasure is reflected in every facet of your life. As a love adept, it is reflected most specifically in your comfort in feeling pleasure, pleasuring yourself, and sharing pleasure during the arts of lovemaking.

"Your next lesson is to explore your relationship to pleasure and the sacred artistry of sex."

Skill 2: Sex as Sacred Artistry

The ancient love sages who undertook the study and practice of the Art of Love in ancient China understood that one's awareness and uses of sex offered ephemeral pleasures but could also provide a sacred tonic for intimate regeneration, lasting intimate fulfillment, and the foundation for lifelong bonding. I have adapted the Tao's teachings of the sages to help you learn to become a love artist and cultivate your own sexuality so that you can engage in these sacred arts. In this skill, we will explore the following: Pleasure, Discover Who You Are Sexually, Expressing Healthy Sexuality, Sexual Healing, Prepare Your Body Temple for Sacred Sexuality, Self-Pleasure, Circulating Sexual Energy, and Sexual Awakening.

Pleasure

Pleasure is that which takes you to the self
Sorrow is what takes you away from the self
>   —Sri Sri Ravi Shankar

Pleasure is important to feeling fulfilled in our romantic relationship and in our overall life experience. Pleasure can increase our health, prolong our life, and help us develop more bonded relationships. In their book, *Healthy Pleasures*, Robert Ornstein, Ph.D., and David Sobel, M.D., write, "From eating to reproduction, from attending to the environment to caring for others, pleasure guides us to better health. Doing what feels right and feeling good are beneficial for health and the survival of the species."

We all seek pleasure, whether we know it or not, because we wish to experience our true self. Pleasure can make us feel joy and the bliss of pure being. Our sensory body naturally receives pleasure through touch, sight, scent, sound, and taste. When we are open to this flow of good feelings, we increase our vitality and deepen our happiness. However, pleasure has the opposite effect on our body and mind if we abuse it.

We can resist the positive feelings of pleasure as a result of many governing cultural beliefs that elevate sacrifice, struggle, punishment, and suffering. For instance, having a dessert is often referred to as a "guilty pleasure." Guilt is the feeling that we have committed a crime or sin. If we think of having dessert as doing something naughty, we will possibly enjoy some pleasure but also feel guilt while we eat the dessert, and we will be left with more guilty feelings afterwards.

As demonstrated in the example above, our relationship to sensual pleasure can feel double sided. On the one hand, it can feel exciting and stimulating to experience pleasure, and at the same time it can bring up guilt, shame, pain, secrecy, and frustration. We may be so accustomed to this dual feeling that we actually don't realize that there is anything abnormal about it.

Shame can cause a strong resistance to taking in bodily pleasure, enjoying emotional love, and living a truly fulfilling life. Each person has a different threshold of pleasure based on the person's earliest beliefs about experiencing pleasure. For instance, if you grew up with parents who often, and happily, demonstrated physical affection, you would naturally be more inclined to feel good about pleasure, which would allow you to want to experience more of it. However, if your parents were critical of your developing body and caused you to become self-conscious and ashamed of your appearance, you could find it difficult and even painful to allow yourself to have physical pleasure.

We may be able to take in a certain amount of pleasure but then shut off from experiencing certain other feelings of pleasure, such as sharing more sexual intimacy, feeling good about ourselves consistently, or having a deeper emotional connection with our lover. When this occurs, the body and heart begin to translate the excess pleasure into emotional or physical pain—causing feelings of anger, grief, or physical numbness—or may bring up a desire to incorporate pain and punishment into our pleasure.

Sex as sacred artistry provides not only great physical pleasure but is a tonic that provides intimate regeneration, lasting intimate fulfillment, and the foundation for life-long bonding. Sex seen as sacred artistry may actually seem taboo or shocking, or it may even bring up fear in you. Check in with yourself and see if you agree with the concept of sex as sacred artistry or whether it makes you feel a little strange and maybe hesitant. We can feel this way when we have long held the idea that sexual pleasure and sacredness do not go hand and hand.

Many religious traditions throughout the ages, including Christianity, Judaism, Islam, Buddhism, and Hinduism, have taught that physical pleasure is actually in conflict with a spiritual path. They have believed that pleasure prevents spiritual development. This idea has created for many people a disconnection between sacredness and enjoying sexual pleasure.

When we hold the belief that sexual pleasure and sacredness are separate, we often act out with negative sexual habits. Some of the most prevalent negative sexual habits are the following:

- Repression—We can constrict our natural sexual expression, causing us to act out in unconscious or distorted ways. For instance, when our belief that sex is bad hinders our ability to reach out and engage in a healthy, intimate sexual relationship, the repression can ultimately erupt, causing us to act out sexually with random and careless promiscuity.

- Hiding Out—We can rely on intoxicating substances to relax and have a good time sexually.

- Rebelling—We can rebel by overindulging in addictive sexual behavior or by acting sexually careless, reckless, or deceptive—for instance, by cheating on our partner.

- Punishing Ourselves—We can bring pain to the body during sex with often glamorized activities like S&M, domination, and acts of repression and self-mutilation.

As we become aware of our belief system about sexual pleasure, we can start to let go of the beliefs that no longer serve us, and we can breathe in new, positive, life-affirming beliefs about pleasure. The most important belief is that integrating pleasure with our heart and spiritual essence is beautiful, exciting, and more fulfilling.

Sacredly pleasuring ourselves—meaning including our whole self in the experience of pleasure—invites us to build a better relationship with our concepts of pleasure. As we discover how to have greater sexual pleasure with ourselves, we alleviate our inner conflict, our longing, our loneliness, and our dependency on a partner to do it for us. This liberates us to experience sexual pleasure all the time, on our own as well as with our partner.

Discover Who You Are Sexually

This section will help you discover who you are sexually, enabling you to experience more fulfillment and happiness in the sexual arena. The more aware you are of your emotions and beliefs around sexuality, the more you can nurture their healthier aspects. Use your journal to support you in this process.

To discover your beliefs about sexual pleasure, ask yourself:

- What positive emotions do I have toward partnering sexually?
- What negative emotions do I have toward partnering sexually?
- Where did these positive and negative emotions originate?
- What do I like best about sexual partnering?
- What do I like the least about sexual partnering?
- Am I more comfortable with the physical or the emotional part of sexual partnering?
- Why?
- Do I like to enjoy self-pleasuring?
- How do I feel being naked?
- How do I feel about being emotionally vulnerable?
- What pleasure do I now want to experience sexually?
- How do I feel after doing this exercise?
- Do I feel vulnerable?
- Do I feel more aware?
- Do I feel excited and ready to claim more of who I want to be sexually?

Wherever you are today, feel good about who you are sexually, and allow this exercise to support you in growing stronger in your sexual identity.

Expressing Healthy Sexuality

Often, our sexual education and behavior stems from watching dysfunctional television characters and witnessing family and friends as confusing examples. It is easy to pick up and mimic our most frequently witnessed sexual behaviors and accept them as the "norm." We may repeat these norms over and over, even when they are unsatisfying and bring us unhappiness. Why? Because most likely we are unclear about how to experience sex in a satisfying, healthy way.

What is healthy sexuality? What does it look like; how does it feel? Healthy sexuality, whether you are single or in a relationship, and regardless of your sexual orientation, carries the same attributes.

The list below includes qualities of a healthy sexual experience. Give yourself the opportunity to think about how healthy your sexuality is, where it may be improved, and what you could add to this list in order to enjoy a healthy sexual experience. If you would like to write about your thoughts in your journal, do so now.

Healthy Sexuality ...

- Replenishes you
- Is respectful of yourself and others
- Opens your heart
- Engages your spirit
- Is sometimes slow, long, and luxurious, and sometimes quick and hot
- Includes variety and fun
- Can be playful, deep and intense, soft, sensuous, and passionate
- Brings mutual pleasure and satisfaction
- Allows you to communicate what is desired, not desired, feels good, doesn't feel good, is too much or too little
- Balances and harmonizes
- Emotionally connects
- Is full of love
- Happens frequently
- Is a conscious agreement between lovers
- Does not include pain, turmoil, power play, or deception
- Leaves behind clarity, openness, happiness, and fulfillment

Choosing a Healthy Sexual Experience

Whether you are having sex for the first time with someone new or having ongoing sex with your intimate partner, you always have the option to choose a healthy sexual experience.

Four Important Questions to Ask Yourself Before Having Sex for the First Time with Someone:

1. *Do you know him or her?* How well do you know this person and for how long?

2. *Is he/she healthy?* Do you know his/her sexual health status?

3. *How's your self-esteem right now?* Are you honoring yourself emotionally, mentally, physically, and spiritually and the other person by making this choice? And will you love yourself by having this sexual experience? Before having sex? During sex? After having sex?

4. *Are you in your right mind?* Are you under the influence of intoxicants that would prevent you from making the right choice?

You may want to carry these questions in your purse or wallet to help you always make the right choice for you. Go to the last page of this book to clip out your own question card.

Three Important Questions to Ask Yourself Before Having Sex in an Ongoing Intimate Relationship:

1. Are my mind, body, heart, and spirit available to be fully present for this interaction?

2. Is my partner also available in this way to be fully present for this interaction?

3. If not, how can I get there or help my partner get there? (You may need to make a mental adjustment, have a talk, give your lover a massage, take a bath together, etc.)

In either case, once you have determined that this will be a healthy sexual experience, the next step is to have conscious, clear dialogue with the person you are about to engage with sexually. Conscious dialogue about sexual health, birth control, and the intentions you both have for interacting sexually—for instance, whether you want to start a relationship, have a hot fling, or enjoy a passionate night of connecting even more fully with your lover—will help you both be clear, comfortable, and able to release your inhibitions to enjoy a healthy sexual interaction.

If this is a first-time experience with a new partner, prior to things heating up, you should discuss your sexual health status, how you will practice safe sex, and how you will conduct your sexual relationship.

If you are in a relationship, it is important to communicate regularly about your sex life. You should periodically discuss what sex means to each of you and how each of you would like to improve your sexual relationship. Without criticism and finger-pointing, discuss having sex more frequently, with more emotional or spiritual connection, more oral sex, more tenderness, and/or more heat. This regular check-in with your lover helps your sexual relationship stay vibrant, up to date, alive, and juicy.

Facing Your Thresholds in Sex

Choosing to experience sexuality in a healthy way often brings up areas of resistance that have been blocking you from experiencing the fullest pleasure, emotional connectedness, and sacredness that you are capable of during sex. Making love in a healthy way can initially bring up past heartache, past sexual trauma, and spiritually disconnected feelings and memories. It can also cause hidden shame to surface.

Facing your thresholds is an important part of the process of becoming sexually healthier, but it is also a step where many people get stuck, hit their wall, and don't go any further. That's when they will begin to think the relationship isn't turning them on anymore. It is important to recognize what is happening. Be soft, allow vulnerabilities and traumas to surface, speak of them, and allow yourself to be supported and held through your resistance. It is important to get to the root of these painful sexual issues. Mending our relationship with our sexuality is at the root of having greater sexual health and more pleasurable sexual experiences. The next section introduces you to the sexual healing process.

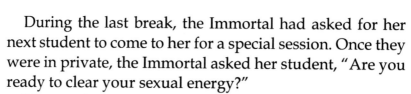

During the last break, the Immortal had asked for her next student to come to her for a special session. Once they were in private, the Immortal asked her student, "Are you ready to clear your sexual energy?"

The student, not expecting this question, contracted physically as old, disturbing memories welled up in her mind.

"Take your time," said the Immortal. "If this is not the right time we can do it—"

"I'm ready," interrupted the student. The young woman, although initially resistant, realized that she felt safe with the teacher and comfortable in the respectful and serene space that was created for this lesson to take place. She also knew that receiving the clearing technique first-hand from her teacher would be a life-changing experience.

The Immortal asked her pupil to lie down upon a long cushion in the grass in front of a fountain shaped like a chalice.

The Immortal sat down beside the student and placed her hand a few inches away from the student's body, above her Sexual Palace. Su Nu closed her eyes to perceive the sexual energy field of the student and began the process of supporting the pupil's sexual clearing.

As she did, she communicated with a gentle voice, "Sexual sensation can be dulled when there has been emotional or physical trauma here."

A tear flowed down the pupil's cheek, mirroring the water that flowed down the sides of the chalice behind her. The Immortal then placed her other hand above the pupil's heart and said, "By connecting sensitively with your Sexual Palace and utilizing your breath, sexual clearing can take place. Heightened sexual sensitivity and vitality can result."

The pupil began to feel the clearing in her Sexual Palace, and a deep serenity settled across her face. The Immortal continued to lovingly support the student until the healing was complete.

Sexual Healing

Many people have suffered from being sexually wounded, both mentally and physically. If we have been wounded sexually, we can disconnect from the sexual pleasure experience through loss of libido, numbness, lack of interest, or by engaging in sexual promiscuity, all in an attempt to avoid our sexual pain or traumas.

For instance, many women and men today suffer from a lack of sexual desire. For many of these individuals, a low libido has deep roots in the widespread religious opinions taught by many of the world religions that I mentioned earlier, that expressed that enjoying sexual pleasure is sinful and inconsistent with a spiritual path. This specific religious doctrine, which can be found in many of the major world religions, has sent harmful effects rippling across generations, creating sexual repression, distorted sexual behavior, and rebellion in countless women and men. Healing the ancient guilt complex within people's formative beliefs about sexuality enhances their ability to express and experience pleasure and have an ecstatic connection within their body, heart, mind, and spirit. This return of sexual acceptance and wholeness also allows for much healthier intimate dynamics between lovers.

Some indications of resurfacing trauma are physical pain and a low libido during intercourse or at other times throughout the day. Heaviness, numbness, or the perception of darkness in the sexual area, lower back, or down the thighs or legs can also indicate sexual trauma. In addition, emotional pain can also surface through feelings of fear, rage, guilt, shame, or self-hatred. These are common feelings associated with sexual trauma. It may seem easier to stay disconnected from our wounds, but holding unprocessed trauma inside ourselves is a great burden on our mental and physical well-being.

Facing the disconnected and fragmented parts of our sexuality can be difficult. When practicing the methods described in Sex as Sacred Artistry, we may uncover or reconnect with emotional or physical sexual traumas. If you have experienced sexual trauma, resurfacing is an important step in the healing process.

Sexual Healing Breath

Purpose:
Focused breathing into the Sexual Palace center can help you connect to, feel, be present with, and heal your sexual self.

Awareness:

The Sexual Palace point is located at the midpoint of the pubic bone for men and at the midpoint between the ovaries for women.

Practice:

- You can lie down or sit up for this practice.
- Place your hands over the Sexual Palace area and begin breathing.
- Breathe in and expand this lower abdominal area.
- Exhale and relax this area.
- Continue this breathing rhythm for several minutes.
- As you breathe in, tune in to the emotions and energy of the Sexual Palace.
- As you exhale, release and clear the energy and emotions present here.
- Continue this breathing pattern for several minutes, clearing and refining the sexual energy.
- Now bring the hands up to the heart in prayer position.
- Feel a current of pleasure moving from the sexual center up toward the heart.
- Feel your heart opening up and sending love back to the sexual center.
- Be present here for several minutes.

By breathing and witnessing your emotions and physical sensations—without judgment— you can let go of them, little by little. Sometimes negative feelings may instantly leave; sometimes they come off, layer by layer, through connecting, healing, and letting go.

In addition:

- Writing about your feelings and sensations from your breathing practice in your journal can bring you greater understanding of your sexual healing process.
- Use the Emotional Alchemy exercise to help clear persistent emotions.
- You may also use the following affirmation to support your sexual healing by repeating it out loud or focusing on it in meditation: *"I accept joy and pleasure fully into my sexuality, my whole body, and my life."*

You may want to continue these exercises for two or three weeks before moving on to the next section. Facing and healing sexual wounds is a very important step in experiencing sexual wholeness and fulfillment.

It takes personal courage and a good support system to achieve the best results when working with sexual trauma. If you feel at any time that the practice is bringing up too much pain or too many emotions, you can stop and resume when you are ready. If overwhelming emotions and pain persist over a two to three week period, it is wise to seek help from a qualified counselor or therapist.

Prepare Your Body Temple for Sacred Sexuality

Your body is your temple that you will utilize to perform sacred rites of love and sexuality. The attention that you demonstrate in taking care of your body can initiate and enrich your experience of sex as sacred artistry. Love your body with nourishing preparation to honor the Sacred Lover in you.

Preparing your body by nourishing, purifying, and enhancing your body's natural attributes will set the right tone for a sacred sexual experience.

Daily Preparation of the Body Temple

Nourish your body with energizing and nutritious foods such as:

Organic fresh vegetables and fruits
Free-range organic meats
Whole grains
Seasonally fresh and local foods.

Exercise your body with an appealing workout routine, such as yoga, martial arts, running, dancing, etc., in order to:

Stay fit and energized
Release toxins
Relax muscles
Let go of tensions.

Cleanse your body to maintain excellent hygiene with:

Hot showers
Brushing and flossing your teeth and tongue
Luxurious baths
Manicures and pedicures
Daily bathing of the genital and anal area.

Enhance your body's magnetic radiance, softness and scent with:

Oils
Moisturizer
Natural fragrances.

Self-Pleasure

From the age of three, I have enjoyed the act of self-pleasuring. I was first introduced to the idea of masturbation by my five-year-old cousin, who was discovering for himself the enjoyment of the friction of the swing set between his legs one sunny afternoon when several cousins and myself were left to play in the backyard. Curious, I followed his example and discovered my own sexual pleasure for the first time. I definitely thought the experience was great and have enjoyed the exploration of pleasuring myself ever since. Of course, my self-pleasuring experiences have matured quite a bit since I was a child. I feel that self-pleasuring is a sacred, healthy, and personal experience for me. In the next several pages, I will introduce you to practices that I have enjoyed integrating into my own self-pleasuring experiences. Now it is time for you to discover them for yourself and find out how you can enjoy sex and pleasure in a whole new way.

A Self-Pleasure Experience

Purpose:
Utilize your touch to discover what you enjoy in regards to your sensual pleasure. Knowledge of what you like and don't like, how to pleasure yourself, and how to communicate what feels good is not only liberating to you but also enhances pleasure and connectivity in your intimate relationship.

Practice:
You can use a mirror, if you like, to help you discover your sexual pleasure and beauty.

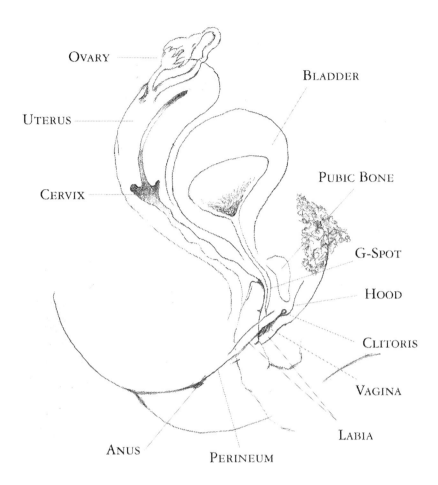

FEMALE GENITALIA

For Women:

Begin to caress your genitalia with your hands and fingers.

Caress the area around the clitoris. This small, sensitive erectile organ between the folds of the labia (external genital lips) is capable of providing intense pleasure.

Clitorises can be exposed or can be very small and challenging to locate within the folds of the labia and hood. Some clitorises are completely hidden under the labia and hood and can't be seen but can be felt. The body of the clitoris projects outward from the pubic bone and generally ranges from two to four centimeters in length. Rub up, down, and around the clitoris. Stroke the area in a circular motion.

Use all your fingers to heighten your sensual circular motion. Apply a pulsing pressure to both sides of the clitoris. If desired, insert a finger into the vaginal entrance, finding your G-spot, and continue to stimulate yourself. For additional arousal, massage your perineum area, located between the vagina and the anus.

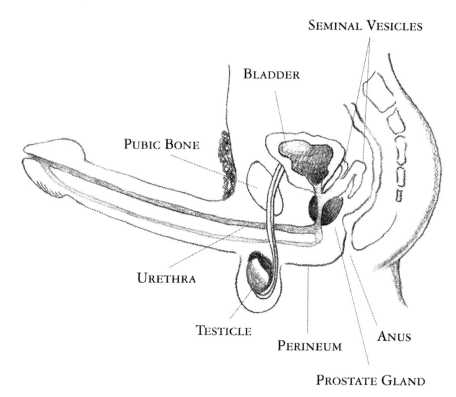

SEMINAL VESICLES

BLADDER

PUBIC BONE

URETHRA

TESTICLE

PERINEUM

ANUS

PROSTATE GLAND

MALE GENITALIA

For Men:

Caress your penis and testicle area. There are many sensitive nerve endings in the penis and testicle area. Enjoy the increased pleasure and stimulation of your erotic touch. Massage up and down the shaft of the penis and around the head, with varying degrees of pressure and speed. Stimulate your testicles with the fingertips.

If desired, massage around the perineum area, between the testicles and the anus. Gently stroke this area with your fingertips for additional arousal. This massage also brings greater vitality to the prostate gland, the rounded gland located in the upper-middle back area of the anal canal.

Pleasure Flow for Women and Men:
As you reach a heightened and satisfying level of sexual pleasure, whether becoming deeply aroused or having an orgasm, use your fingers and hands to caress this feeling of pleasure into your face, hips, and torso. Move your pleasure from between your thighs to all over your body.

Notice what touch and pressure and in which areas feels most pleasing to you. Feel your self-pleasure nourishing you deeply and fully.

Breath of Pleasure

Breathing is fundamental to the Art of Love. Why? Because breathing allows you to skillfully move energy throughout your body and your energy centers to enhance pleasure. If you have ever felt frustrated and let down by your experience of sexual pleasure or are ready to catapult your sexual excitement and pleasure to a whole new level, this is a wonderful skill for you to cultivate.

Breath of Pleasure

Purpose:
The Breath of Pleasure practice is the primary sacred breathing practice of Tao love artisans.

Pleasure breathing intensifies your personal pleasure while providing the foundation for Sacred Love-Making with your lover. The Breath of Pleasure refines the quality and sensitivity of your sexual energy that offers a variety of benefits to both men and women including toning the sexual organs—which prevents premature ejaculation in men and increases arousal for women. This breathing practice also improves the enjoyment of receiving and giving pleasure as well as increases both sexual and overall health.

Practice:

Step One for Women:
- Bring the tongue up to touch the upper palate.
- Smile inwardly.
- Feel your mind and body relaxing.

- Combine a long, slow breath with a gentle contraction and opening of the vagina to enhance pleasure.
- Imagine the labia (lips of vagina) as the petals of a flower.
- Breathe in and gently close the labia and vagina with your mind and a small contraction of your muscles.
- Exhale.
- Gently relax and allow the labia to fold out in the opposite direction.
- Rest momentarily.
- Repeat for several minutes.

Caution:
Do not practice this breathing exercise if you are menstruating, for it may hinder the completion of the bleeding process. Also, women should not practice if they have a bladder or vaginal infection; the exercise can further aggravate the infection.

Step One for Men:
- Bring the tongue up to touch the upper palate.
- Smile.
- Feel your mind and body relaxing.
- Breathe into your Sexual Palace to experience a deeper sexual connection.
- As you breathe in, draw the testicles upwards.
- Gently close the tip of the penis with your mind and a small contraction of the muscles.
- Exhale.
- Let these areas relax completely.
- Gently direct this movement (or contraction) with your mind and a little muscle.
- Repeat this breathing pattern for several minutes.

*Men can repeat this exercise up to 100 times a day to strengthen ejaculation control.

Caution:
Men should not practice if they have a bladder infection.

Step Two, Breathing Pleasure into the Pelvic Bowl for Both Women and Men:

- Inhale and contract the genitals. Draw your awareness up from the genitals into the region of the sexual/pelvic cavity. (This is an expansion of the Sexual Palace)
- Fill the area with the Breath of Pleasure, from the front of the hipbones to the back at the sacrum, the triangular bone structure forming the back base of the pelvis.
- Hold your breath.
- Exhale and relax.
- Each time, contract the genitals on the inhale and relax fully on the exhale.
- Feel the urogenital muscles—the muscle group located at the base of the body from the frontal genital area through the perineum to the anus—becoming stronger as you practice.
- Feel energy and sexual pleasure expanding through the pelvic cavity.
- Repeat for several minutes until you feel sexual energy expanding throughout the pelvic region.
- Relax your genital muscles completely and enjoy.

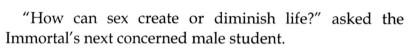

"How can sex create or diminish life?" asked the Immortal's next concerned male student.

Su Nu answered, "Sexual energy utilized and channeled properly restores health and emotional well-being and promotes longevity. Sex used improperly can deplete a person's life force, causing disharmony and illness.

"A master of the Art of Love learns to turn the wheel of creation to cultivate and circulate their sexual energy. Thereafter, this sacred art grants them the ultimate health and energy tonic. The vital organs become stronger, blood circulation increases, the immune system improves, and the body and mind enjoys greater fulfillment."

The Immortal took another sip of her elixir as she gently petted her golden boa, curled up beside her, while he affectionately hissed, flittering his tongue in agreement.

"What is the wheel of creation?" the excited and curious young man asked.

"Ah," said the Immortal. "The wheel of creation is a specific pathway within your body. If you want to become a master love artisan, you must learn to open and turn it. In this lesson you will learn to cultivate and circulate sexual energy through this pathway.

"Circulating your sexual energy through the wheel of creation will unlock the secrets to greater health, sexual ecstasy, and fulfillment."

Circulating Sexual Energy

Pleasure is becoming intense vibration and forgetting that you are matter.
　—Unknown

Long held as Traditional Chinese Medicine's wheel of life, the Microcosmic Orbit is made up of two energy meridians that form a circuit. The governing vessel meridian begins at the base of the body and moves up the spine to the crown of the head and down to the palate of the mouth. The conception vessel meridian moves from the palate of the mouth down the front of the torso to the base of the body.

The Microcosmic Orbit receives its name from the Taoist idea that our personal orbit and the greater cosmic orbit of stars and planets are in correlation and share an intimate relationship. When we learn how to clear and mobilize the energy of our orbit, we can gain greater attunement with nature and the universe. This orbit's pathway, when it is clear and open, nourishes all the systems of the mind and body.

If you have ever visited a Chinese acupuncturist, it is very possible that you received a needle in the top of the head or in another energy center along this pathway, which would have benefited your health by activating a steady flow of energy throughout your Microcosmic Orbit. In the practice of circulating sexual energy, we will utilize the Microcosmic Orbit to circulate sexual energy throughout the body.

Circulating sexual energy through the orbit has remained a revered and secret practice of the Chinese love masters, passed down for thousands of years. Traditionally, the practice remained hidden until a student proved their dedication by studying the arts for many years. For only when they possessed the wisdom and skill to grasp the movement of energy through the Microcosmic Orbit could they utilize the practice properly.

Throughout the world's varied mythologies, the snake has, for millennia, symbolized the journey of the awakening sexual energy, and the tree has represented the sexual energy's travel itinerary and destination. The sexual energy (snake), once awakened at the base of the spine, travels sensually up the spine (tree), to the crown of the head and beyond. This erotic journey would arouse pleasure, move that pleasure through the body, enlighten the energy centers, and merge body with spirit, creating a state of sacred union and ecstasy.

Even though you may not have years of study of the Art of Love under your belt, it is important to realize that circulating sexual energy is very powerful. Utilize it wisely to promote mutual pleasure and well-being for both yourself and your lover.

Building upon the Breath of Pleasure, this second sacred sexual practice expands your own experience of sexual pleasure to reach your entire body. Simultaneously, learning to circulate sexual energy increases health, vitality, and harmony. Achieving the circulation of sexual energy is also the basis for reaching multiple orgasms, higher states of ecstasy, and having a closer spiritual union with your lover.

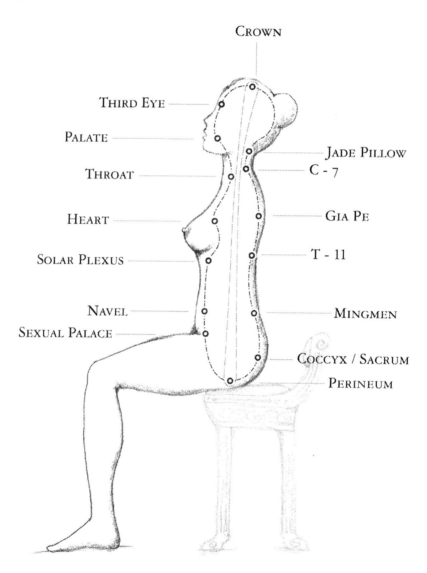

MICROCOSMIC ORBIT

Names of the Centers Along the Microcosmic Orbit
In the illustration, you see the proper Taoist terms for each center. Below, I have included the correlating names for each energy center, which describe the essence that each center represents.

- Navel   Center of Nourishment
- Sexual Palace   Center of Pleasure
- Perineum   Center of Earth/Wealth
- Coccyx/Sacrum   Center of Support
- Mingmen   Door of Life
- T-11   Back of Power Center
- Gia-Pe   Back of Emotional Center
- C-7   Back of Communication Center
- Jade Pillow   Mind-Meets-Body Center
- Crown   Spiritual Center
- Third Eye   Psychic Center
- Palate   Connective Center
- Throat   Front of Communication Center
- Heart   Emotional Center
- Solar Plexus   Front of Power Center

Circulating Sexual Energy

Purpose:
Experiencing sexual circulation involves utilizing the Breath of Pleasure in combination with mindful focus to circulate sexual energy through the Microcosmic Orbit. Energy floods the body with sexual hormones and ignites the experience of full-body pleasure and ecstasy.

I recommend opening the centers of the Microcosmic Orbit prior to circulating sexual energy by spending time focusing on each center for one minute and then linking the centers together by visualizing a golden cord. You may want to do this for several days or weeks before attempting to move your sexual energy through the pathway. Because the following practice will magnify whatever emotions the sexual energy connects with, it is a good idea to clear and calm the mind and body emotionally with the Emotional Alchemy practice in Skill One prior to doing this practice.

Preparation

I recommend beginning by sitting up straight in a cross-legged position on a pillow or in a chair, with your feet planted firmly on the floor. As you become more comfortable with circulating your sexual energy, you may try it lying down. Note: As with the Breath of Pleasure, do not practice if you are menstruating or suffering from a bladder or vaginal infection.

Begin the Breath of Pleasure by bringing the tongue up to touch the upper palate and then smile inwardly.

Women: Gently breathe in and close the vagina with your mind and a little muscle. Then exhale and let it open and relax. Repeat this breathing pattern several times to connect to your sexual energy.

Men: Gently breathe in and draw up the testicles and close the tip of the penis. Exhale and let these areas relax. Repeat this breathing pattern several times to connect to your sexual energy.

For Women and Men:

- Begin to refine and cultivate your sexual energy.
- On the inhale of the Breath of Pleasure, visualize sipping up sexual energy (like you would through a straw) to one center at a time along the Microcosmic Orbit. On the first breath, you will start at the Sexual Palace, moving toward the perineum. Then on each new breath, move your sexual energy to each center along the back of the spine. (You are directing the breath from the bottom of the spine upward toward the crown.)
- Hold your breath and your sexual energy for a few seconds at each center.
- Then exhale and bring your awareness back to the Sexual Palace center before continuing on to the next center.
- In the beginning, I recommend focusing on only one or several centers from the illustration, rather than on all of them.
- As you become more familiar with the practice, you can move through all the centers in one practice session.

Practice:

Sip Sex to the Perineum or Earth/Wealth Center:

- Inhale the Breath of Pleasure and contract, drawing the sexual energy from the genitals back to the perineum (the point between the genitals and anus).
- Feel the sexual energy expanding from the Sexual Palace to the perineum.
- Hold your breath for several seconds at the perineum.
- Exhale.
- Relax, drawing your awareness back to the Sexual Palace.

Sip Sex to the Coccyx or Center of Support:

- Inhale the Breath of Pleasure again.
- Draw the sexual energy to the coccyx, the tip of the tailbone.
- Hold your breath there. Feel the energy rising.
- Hold for several seconds.
- Exhale.
- Relax, bringing the awareness back to the Sexual Palace.

Sip Sex to the Mingmen or Door of Life:

- Inhale. Contract the genitals.
- Draw the sexual energy to the Mingmen, the back of the navel on the spine.
- Hold.
- Exhale. Relax your muscles.
- Let your awareness flow back to the sexual organs.
- Smile.

Sip Sex to the T-11 or Back of the Power Center:

- Draw the breath and sexual energy to the back of the solar plexus, or T-11.
- Hold.
- Feel pleasure ascending the spine.
- Exhale. Relax.

Sip Sex to the Gia-Pe or Back of the Emotional Center:

- **Note:** It is not necessary to stop at this point along the orbit. If you choose to stop here, make sure that you have cleared your emotions to a great degree (see Emotional Alchemy) so that energy can easily and safely move through this center.
- Draw the breath and sexual energy to the Gia-Pe, or back of the Heart Center.
- Hold.
- Feel pleasure ascending the spine.
- Exhale. Relax.

Sip Sex to the C-7 or Back of the Communication Center:

- Breathe in from the genitals to the C-7 at the base of the neck.
- Hold for several seconds.
- Then exhale and relax.
- Allow the sexual energy to descend back down the spine.

Sip Sex to the Jade Pillow or Mind-Meets-Body Center:

- Inhale and contract the genitals.
- Draw pleasure to the jade pillow, the base of the skull.
- Hold your sexual energy here.
- Exhale. Relax.

Sip Sex to the Crown or Spiritual Center:

- Now take in a deep Breath of Pleasure.
- Draw sexual energy to the crown, the very top of the head.
- Feel the sexual energy merging with the spiritual energy.
- Hold and then exhale.

Let Sex Flow Through Your Full Body:

And allow the sexual energy to flow down the front of your body through the following areas:

- Mid-eyebrow area, or Psychic Center
- To the Palate at the top of the mouth, or Connection Center
- Down to the Throat Center, or Front of Communication Center
- Then to the Heart Center, or Emotional Center

- To the Solar Plexus, or Front of Power Center
- To the Navel, or Center of Nourishment
- And, finally, to the Sexual Palace, or Pleasure Center.

Feel the sensation of sexual energy vibrating all over the body. In the beginning, you may feel that you are using a lot of muscle power, but gradually, you will use less muscle and more mind and breath power. You can stop here or continue on. If you decide to stop here, utilize the completion step to do so.

Now Circulate Sexual Energy (the snake) Through the Orbit (the tree) on One Breath:

- Practice the Breathe of Pleasure for several minutes.
- Begin to cultivate your sexual energy on one breath.
- On the inhale of the Breath of Pleasure, sip up sexual energy from the Sexual Palace up to the crown of the head.
- Hold your breath and sexual energy at the crown for several seconds.
- Exhale.
- Smile as you let the energy flow down the front of the Microcosmic Orbit back to the Sexual Palace.
- Repeat the sequence nine times.
- After you have completed the ninth rotation, relax and enjoy the sensation of bringing yourself into full-body sexual pleasure. This may or may not resemble your normal climax. Neither does it require male ejaculation.
- Feel a current of sexual energy moving along the pathway from the Sexual Palace to the crown and back to the Sexual Palace again.
- Safely store the sexual energy (coiled snake) from this practice in the dantien, the main energy reservoir located approximately two inches below the navel, by circling the hands at the area below the navel.
- Relax and enjoy the pleasure of cultivating your sacred sexual artistry.

Completion Step:

Complete this practice by brushing the hands down from the top of the head along the front of the body to the dantien underneath the navel. Rub your hands in a circle at the dantien to ground your energy and prevent side effects such as nausea, hot flashes, or headaches.

Sexual Awakening

This sexual artistry practice is for the purpose of achieving sexual awakening within yourself. It is about having your own integral experience of sexual pleasure, ecstasy, and communion with the divine.

This is a very pleasing sexual experience, but even more than that, it is a deeply spiritual, healing, integrative, and creative experience. The following practice of sexual awakening is one that I often enjoy to connect me with the experience of the sacred through my sexuality.

Sexual Awakening Experience

Purpose:
Sexual awakening offers us the experience of sacred pleasure. This is achieved by utilizing the Breath of Pleasure to draw the cultivated sexual energy up the core channel of your body through the midpoint of each of the energy centers. Doing so will clear your central channel and draw your sexual energy upwards—merging and expanding your connectivity with ecstasy and wholeness.

Practice:

- Begin to pleasure yourself, touching yourself sexually to bring yourself into a state of arousal.
- Begin the Breathe of Pleasure, gently contracting the genitals and relaxing them.
- On one long, slow, deep breath, draw your sexual energy up the center of the inside of your body: Up through your abdominal area (the center of nourishment), through the solar plexus (the center of power), through the heart (the emotional center), through the throat (the center of clarity and communication), through the third eye (the psychic center), and through the crown of the head (the spiritual center).
- Feel the wave of pleasure traveling up your core channel and opening you up to your greater self.
- Perceive the energy centers becoming more open and lighter and the sexual, heart, and spiritual energies connecting in a sacred union.
- Ride this wave of pleasure and ecstasy.
- Feel the wave of pleasure expanding your body awareness and feel a sense of merging with the divine.

- Exhale.
- Continue repeating the breathing cycle for several minutes with relaxation in between.
- Rest in a state of bliss, love, and sacred union.
- Always finish this practice by collecting the energy underneath the navel at the dantien to avoid excess energy from collecting in your head, which may cause nausea or dizziness. Spiral with the hands around the dantien. You may even want to get up and walk around to ground your energy.
- Rest.

For this next set of Sacred Lover lessons, Su Nu would teach two students simultaneously. As her next students came to join her under a willow tree in the garden, the Immortal choose to give them the freedom to decide what the lesson would be. Su Nu asked her students to sit with her on the blanket under the tree.

"Become aware of the question that is most pressing for you right now," instructed Su Nu. "When the question comes, you may ask it."

After several minutes, a young woman spoke. "Teacher, how do I know if a potential partner is really my Sacred Lover?"

Su Nu replied, "First you must know how to recognize a Sacred Lover.

"A Sacred Lover is an individual who cultivates qualities of love in their intimate relationships. A Sacred Lover is someone who delights in a soulful connection as much as the sexual and emotional connection in a relationship.

"When you are cultivating the skills of a Sacred Lover on an ongoing basis, experiencing Sacred Love follows naturally. In a shut-off state due to feelings of inadequacy, you will have a difficult time drawing in the right relationship. You may settle for a relationship that will not provide the real love, nurturing, and intimacy that you desire.

"However, there are several things you can remember to help you welcome Sacred Love into your life. First, take time to qualify an intimate partner. Don't rush the process of courtship. Find out more about whom a potential partner really is and if you are a match before entering the relationship.

"Secondly, choose a partner who easily respects, supports, and nourishes your whole self. Notice how the person speaks to you and how he treats you. Does being with him feel nurturing to you? Is he kind and respectful to you and to others? Be wary of seduction and glamour. Meet his friends. You can often discover who a potential partner is by who he has close to him."

"If I am a Sacred Lover, is it necessary that the partner I choose be a Sacred Lover?" asked a young man.

After a long moment of silence, the Immortal replied, "It depends on what kind of love experience you want to have. While an average lover is usually adept in a few areas of intimacy, the whole person is rarely met. A Sacred Lover enjoys greater pleasure, deeper emotional union, and a soul connection in intimate partnering."

The young man nodded.

Su Nu continued. "It is always your decision what kind of love experience to have. Your willingness to take the journey of self-discovery and make new relationship choices will lead you to the treasure of sacred partnership."

Skill 3: How to Identify a Sacred Lover

Actualizing a sacred love relationship that allows us to be a whole person and deeply nurtures our essence and our life is our birthright. However, finding such a relationship can be challenging. Discerning qualities in prospective lovers and developing the lover within us are keys to the true connection that all of us seek. In this vital chapter you will learn how to identify a sacred partner in the following sections: What Does Sacred Love Look and Feel Like?; Characteristics of a Sacred Lover; Discover What You Want for Sacred Partnership; Perform the Inner Marriage to Attract Your Sacred Lover; Get Out and Attract Your Sacred Lover; Choose a Sacred Lover with the Wisdom of a Love Artisan; Beware of the Illusion of Sacred Partnership; and how to Choose Your Sacred Lover Again and Again.

What Does Sacred Love Look and Feel Like?

The experience of a Sacred Love relationship is one of alignment: a feeling of alignment within yourself and with someone else. It is not two halves becoming a whole, but your whole person meeting another whole person. It is a feeling of correct connection with another human being. It is a meeting of equals and a resonating harmony between persons. It is an experience of joyful chemistry, sharing, understanding, and growing into your truest *you* with someone.

Emotionally, Sacred Love feels like generosity in your capacity to give love and receptivity to the abundance of love your loved one has to give. It feels like words are not required, yet verbal communication is shared easily. Emotionally, Sacred Love is supportive, joyful, and passionate.

Physically, Sacred Love looks and feels like sexual chemistry and electrical connectivity with another person. It feels mutually pleasing, nurturing, and even ecstatic.

Mentally, Sacred Love feels stimulating, unifying, and growth oriented as you share complementary ideas, viewpoints, and intentions for your life.

Spiritually, Sacred Love looks and feels like kindredness that is beyond the mental and physical connection. It feels as though there is an organic closeness, understanding, respect, and knowledge of each other. And there is a natural agreement to grow as human beings, awakening and sharing consciously together.

Nurturing the lover within you enhances your personal comprehension of love that will increase your skill of discernment. I have created this next set of exercises to help you discover where you are in your process of development as a lover and to help you more easily identify and attract your Sacred Lover into your life.

Characteristics of a Sacred Lover

This is a great questionnaire for singles to discover what to look for in a relationship and to support couples in making their relationship stronger. If you are in a partnership, ask your partner to join you and then discuss your findings with each other.

Use the checklist below to identify the Sacred Lover characteristics in you and discover the qualities needed for a sacred partnership. You can make this exercise an entry in your journal. Check the first space beside the qualities that you already have. Decide how developed that quality is in you by writing a number from one to ten in the second space, one being the least and ten being the greatest. For the characteristics you are still working on or would like to begin developing, write in your journal about how you can achieve them.

Yes   **Scale 1-10**

            (10 being greatest)

Yes	Scale 1-10	
_____	_____	**Readiness to experience a healthy intimate relationship**
_____	_____	**Capacity to know what I want and need to feel loved**
_____	_____	**Ability to have honest and healthy communication**
_____	_____	**Confidence in giving love and affection to my lover**
_____	_____	**Confidence in feeling that I am loveable**
_____	_____	**Respect and love for myself in the relationship**
_____	_____	**Respect for my lover with my words**
_____	_____	**Respect for my lover with my behaviors**
_____	_____	**Ability to appreciate my lover**
_____	_____	**Ability to have an ongoing, healthy sexual connection with my lover**
_____	_____	**Capacity to listen**
_____	_____	**Ability to find resolution in disagreements**
_____	_____	**Ability to reflect on my part in a disagreement or conflict**
_____	_____	**Capacity to be emotionally present**
_____	_____	**Courage to stay present during life challenges for me, my partner, or the relationship**
_____	_____	**Willingness to share responsibilities and create a relationship of partnership and equality**
_____	_____	**Willingness to have a spiritual connection with my lover**
_____	_____	**Commitment to sustaining a healthy and fulfilling intimate relationship**

Now that you have discovered the characteristics of a Sacred Lover, you should have a better understanding of where you are in your development as a lover and what you can contribute or are contributing to a relationship. You know what you need to work on in yourself in order to enjoy a more fulfilling relationship. You can utilize the exercises throughout Part One: The Sacred Lover to support you in your development of these characteristics. And you now have this essential list of qualities to help you more clearly identify a sacred partner.

Discover What You Want for Sacred Partnership

Now that you have identified where you are in your development as a lover, and the qualities to look for in identifying a Sacred Lover, it is time to discover your most personal, deepest partnership desires. Clarifying what you want for a sacred partnership takes you much closer to manifesting the right relationship for you. Couples can also utilize this practice to clarify what areas of their relationship they want to grow in.

In your journal, make a discovery list of other personal characteristics that describe your Sacred Lover in addition to the ones listed in the last section. When we are only partially aware of what we want and need—or do not believe we can have what we really want in a love relationship—we tend to fall into relationships that meet only a few of our desires. Making a Sacred Lover list helps to attract a more complete and loving union.

Here's how:

- Identify what you are looking for in a sacred partner—most specifically, how you want to connect emotionally, sexually, mentally, and spiritually.

- List the inner qualities that you most need and desire for a nourishing, loving partnership. For example, some inner qualities could include shared values, emotional communication style, level of maturity and sexual chemistry.

- List the external qualities that you most need and desire in a nurturing, loving partnership. External qualities could include alignment with worldly aspirations, family desires, and lifestyle compatibility.

- Take pleasure in reading your Sacred Lover list out loud on a daily basis. If you are single, visualize your Sacred Lover in your life. If you are in a relationship, discuss with your lover how you can meet more of the needs and desires you each want in your relationship.

Perform the Inner Marriage to Attract Your Sacred Lover

Based upon our formative parental and familiar role models of women and men, we develop an internal image of female and male. Many of the challenges we face in creating a healthy, fulfilling intimate relationship stem from how our inner feminine and our inner masculine operate within us. If our male role models were healthy, then our inner masculine image will be healthy. If our male role models were off balance, shut down, critical, untrustworthy, or in any other way dysfunctional, our inner masculine image will reflect those qualities too. In the same way, our inner feminine image will reflect what we learned from our female role models.

The love relationship we attract depends on what inner image we carry of the male and female—and the relationship between the two. This is why the age-old saying that we all marry our mother or father is largely true; even though we may want to get far away from the mother or father personality that we grew up with, we can't help but be drawn to the image of what we carry inside. We can be attracted to the positive traits of our parental figures, but we can also be drawn to their negative traits, because we are compelled to heal the specific parts of ourselves that were wounded during childhood. This is why we end up choosing a mate based on this inner masculine/feminine experience and feeling state.

That said, we can learn how to transform the masculine and feminine images that we carry inside of ourselves. By developing a healthier, unified image of the masculine and feminine we can attract the love we want. The next practice is designed to help do just that.

The Inner Marriage

Purpose:
Develop a healthier image of the masculine and feminine within you.

Practice:
- Sit in a quiet place.
- Close your eyes and visualize your inner feminine—what she looks like, how she acts, how she communicates, how she feels to you.
- Does this inner feminine image match the experiences that you are demonstrating or receiving from the feminine aspect (either in a woman or a man) in your intimate relationship or in past relationships?
- Do you enjoy the qualities and experiences that your inner feminine provides?

- If not, visualize the new qualities that would make your inner feminine a queen to you. See and feel her with your imagination, and give her life.

- Now visualize your inner masculine—what he looks like, how he acts, how he communicates, how he feels to you.

- Does this masculine image match the experiences that you are demonstrating or receiving from the masculine aspect (either in a woman or a man) in your intimate relationship or in past relationships?

- Do you enjoy the qualities and experiences that your inner masculine provides?

- If not, visualize the new qualities that would make your inner masculine a king to you. See and feel him with your imagination, and give him life.

- Now visualize the improved inner masculine and feminine in you, meeting each other face to face and joining in union.

- Feel the new masculine and the new feminine begin to create a marriage.

- Feel this new inner masculine and feminine enter your thoughts, heart, and physical body.

- Feel the sensations of this new union pulsing positive life energy, love, harmony, and health through you.

- Relax and enjoy the sensation of marrying your masculine and feminine anew.

- Repeat the sequence whenever needed.

Once your internal feminine and masculine are operating from a place of health, unity, and wholeness, you will find that your outer relationship will reflect the true essence of the marriage that you desire—which is a harmonious, happy, and sacred union.

Get Out and Attract Your Sacred Lover

Now that you have identified what you want in a relationship, what characteristics your Sacred Lover possesses, and have married your inner masculine and feminine energies, it is time to get out, have fun, and make the right choices for yourself in love!

Here's how:

- Venture out and meet great people.
- Explore new social groups that resonate with you.
- Meet the friends of those couples who exemplify the qualities that you are looking for in a partnership.
- Socialize with people who are involved in activities that reflect your passions.
- Travel to a new area of town or even another city to connect with people who share your same lifestyle interests.
- Get on the Internet and sign up to meet new people on a wonderful dating site.
- At home, surround yourself with inspirational media, including films, art, and music that represent great love relationships.

Choose a Sacred Partner with the Wisdom of a Love Artisan

When you meet a potential Sacred Lover, be diligent about making wise choices that are in alignment with what you deeply need and desire for sacred partnership. Love artisans do not waste time with a partner who will be unable to meet them with the same desire, ability, and willingness to create the love they seek.

Be aware that you will be able to discern certain matching and non-matching qualities right away, both intuitively and cognitively. These qualities include sexual chemistry, sense of humor, worldly aspirations, and lifestyle compatibility. Other aspects will take more time to decipher—for example, the consistent expression of love and respect, the compatibility of shared values, and the level of inner development.

Learn to Choose a Partner with Your Intuitive Wisdom

Intuition is our knowledge of someone or something based on what we sense or feel prior to gathering all the facts. This is one of our greatest allies in choosing the right partner. Learning to quickly scan a potential partner with our intuitive emotional body wisdom develops a heightened skill of discernment.

Our intuition speaks through our body's intelligence. The body speaks to us every day about what is going on in our surroundings and our life. It is an invaluable tool in making the right decisions—if we learn how to tune into it.

Each of us can remember an intuitive feeling that has prevented us from danger. That intuitive or gut feeling comes from sensations in the body.

First intuitions can be right, but we often forget them quickly. Our bodies communicate to us if someone is the right match for us. They also let us know if the responses we receive from our lover make us feel good about ourselves or not. For instance, we may feel openness in our heart if we feel comfortable and connected to someone. We may also feel sexually aroused if we are attracted to someone. But if something or someone isn't right for us, we may experience a twinge in the belly or tightness in our throat or heart, as a warning.

Trust your own knowing of what feels right for you and what doesn't. Don't be afraid to question your perceptions. You will most often find out that there is validity to your hunches.

Upon meeting a potential partner, be aware of your first intuitions. Intuitively read the potential partner's energy field to detect if you resonate with each other's vibration or not. Notice if there is a connection on an emotional, physical, mental, and spiritual level.

Use your body sensations, emotions, and awareness of lightness, openness, and resistance to quickly discern if there is a potential for partnership.

Building Trust in Your Intuitive Wisdom

Purpose:

Learning to tune in and verify your perceptions helps you gain trust in your intuitive wisdom and make wiser decisions for yourself.

Practice:

Tune in when you are with a date or partner. Notice your feelings and sensations, and ask yourself whether you feel good with him or her, and where those good feelings arise. It may be in one or more particular areas, such as your mind, your heart, or your sexuality.

Tune In Emotionally

Become aware of the openness or tightness in a potential partner's heart area. Notice your emotional sensations when you are around him or her. Ask yourself:

- Do I feel I can open up my heart to this person, or do I feel it would be difficult to open up to this person?
- Do I feel emotionally at ease or uncomfortable?
- Do we possess the same capacity to share love?

Tune In Physically and Sexually

Check in to see if you feel sexual chemistry. Often, it is immediate. If it is not immediate, focus intuitively on the flow of energy around the person's pelvis to determine if you feel sexual chemistry and at what level. Then tune in and ask yourself:

- Do I feel good in my body?
- Will sex be passionate?
- Will it be satisfying?
- Will sex create well-being?
- Will it be dramatic?
- Will is be chaotic?
- Will sex create disharmony in my life?
- Will our capacity to explore a sexual relationship together be mutually fulfilling?

Tune In Mentally and Spiritually

Check in to see if you and your potential partner have similar openness and direction in your thoughts and beliefs. You can energetically read your partner by focusing on the energy around his or her forehead and then ask yourself:

- Do I resonate and feel relaxed around this person?
- Do I feel the two of us having stimulating mental and soulful dialogue together?
- Do I feel bored?
- Do we have little to talk about?
- Do I feel heaviness, conflict, or drama?
- Do I feel good in my mind?
- Do I feel good in my spirit?
- Do I feel that this person shares complementary views and a similar capacity to share and enjoy with me in the mental, spiritual, emotional and physical areas?

After going on a date or spending time with your partner, write down how you felt based on the questions above.

A Sacred Lover should feel a positive intuitive connection physically, emotionally, mentally, and spiritually in order to enjoy intimate fulfillment with a partner. As you practice, it will become easier and even fun to discern and adhere to the intuitive wisdom your body offers you every day.

Choosing a Sacred Partner with Your Cognitive Wisdom

Take your time determining whether this person truly qualifies as your Sacred Lover before committing to an intimate relationship. Ask questions. Become your own love investigator. Discover if this really is the right relationship for you.

Here are some questions to help you make the right choices:

- What is important to this person emotionally, sexually, mentally, and spiritually?
- Are his/her priorities compatible with what is important to me?
- Do his/her words and actions match?
- Is this person consistent in how he/she treats and communicates with me?
- In what ways is the communication healthy or unhealthy?

- How does he/she treat others in his/her life?

- How does this person handle a disagreement?

- How does he/she manage life challenges?

- What is this person's idea of fun and adventure?

- What activities does he/she make a priority on a weekly basis? Does he/she include me?

- What has this person been committed to over a long period of time?

- Where is success visible in his/her life? Where is there movement toward success in his/her life? Some examples are: inner development, healthy family relationships and friendships, fulfilling career, strong finances, and ongoing contribution to the community.

- In what areas is this person interested in growing and stretching him/herself?

- Do this person's friends exhibit qualities that I respect and appreciate?

Once you have the answers to your questions, write about them in your journal for more clarity.

Beware of the Illusion of a Sacred Partnership

One of the challenges that you may face in choosing the right relationship is determining whether this person shares your same capacity for creating a sacred partnership. Many of us have experienced a relationship that in the beginning we believe to be perfect for us. We are *so* "in love". It is magical. We seem to connect on every level. And then, three months, six months, a year, or even two years later, the partner is unable to keep loving in the same way, stay physically engaged, or share a soul connection.

This challenge can arise when one person has reached his or her capacity in a specific area of the relationship and lacks the skills to move further. Examples of how this may manifest in a relationship are emotional shutdown, physical disinterest, looking outside of the relationship for emotional connection or sexual passion, or neglecting the relationship.

This experience can be incredibly frustrating and painful to you if you do have the capacity to keep loving, be sexually passionate, and maintain a soul connection. This is why it is wise to discover whether you and your partner share a similar capacity to love each other prior to beginning a relationship.

Determining if you have a similar or equal capacity in your skill as lovers will help you make a clear choice about whether this is the right relationship for you. If you enter a relationship where you and your partner have similar capacities, then the relationship will tend toward greater ease and harmony. You and your partner will share the skills to deal with challenges that arise. If you enter a relationship where you do not share similar capacities for love, the partner that has the greater capacity for it slides into a teacher role. While that may stimulate both partners at first, after some time your relationship will confront challenges and resistances when the less capable partner reaches a relationship threshold and has difficulty moving forward.

While we all face intimacy thresholds in love, sharing a capacity to move through them with skill and love can make our relationship thrive. If not, the relationship will likely struggle and decline. When you or your partner face a challenging intimacy threshold, utilize the processes presented throughout this book to help you move through them more quickly and easily.

Choose Your Sacred Lover Again and Again

Once you have found your Sacred Lover and commit to a sacred partnership, moment-to-moment choices are vital to maintaining an ongoing sacred relationship. Fun, basic practices and activities can and will replenish your relationship.

Choose your Sacred Lover again and again by:

- Making time for romance
- Committing to sexual, emotional, and soulful connectivity with each other on a weekly basis
- Communicating love, respect, appreciation, and truthfulness with each other
- Finding creative ways to celebrate your union
- Resolving issues that arise as quickly as possible
- Nurturing healthy growth in your relationship
- Focusing on what is positive in each other
- Loving the imperfect areas in each other, transforming them into the gifts they are meant to be

THE TALENT OF LOVING ANOTHER
ANOTHER
PART TWO

The Talent of Loving Another will help you develop the essential talents for creating, enjoying, and sustaining a passionate, healthy, and loving relationship with the one you love.

Our Evolving Love Relationships

We are continually discovering what we need in order to experience a fulfilling intimate relationship. From pursuing one another sexually based on primal animal instincts, to considering and connecting emotionally with our hearts, to engaging with each other soul to soul, we are exploring the possibilities of connecting to one another more fully and with greater satisfaction.

An evolution in relationships is occurring worldwide. Women are tapping into their masculine qualities by gaining a powerful external presence and developing financial independence, which empowers them in making their own decisions and supporting their families. Men are also opening up to their more feminine and inner qualities, expressing more openness and sensitivity as well as participating in such activities as caring for children and expressing creativity.

These changes in men and women are progressively filtering into our intimate relationships. We are beginning to relate differently with each other. Men are becoming increasingly more comfortable with expressing emotions and vulnerability. Women are asserting themselves more and speaking up about what is important to them and what they need in intimacy. These developing qualities are bringing men and women toward a more equal playing field, one free of hierarchy and submissiveness and brimming with creativity and true partnership potential.

At their core, relationships are a sacred path. When we are in any partnership, but most dramatically in an intimate relationship, we are given the opportunity to see a reflection of ourselves. Some aspects we like. Some we do not. We attract our partners to us to discover and become more conscious of these particular parts of ourselves. With this awareness, we can more easily see each experience in our relationship as ultimately a way of recognizing the best of ourselves. Our partnerships can also give us greater clarity and support in nurturing and improving those aspects of ourselves that are not yet fully developed. This powerful evolutionary relationship process can allow us to experience who we truly are—the essence of love, oneness, and bliss.

The teacher began her first lesson of the day with two couples. She would be teaching each couple the Talent of Loving Another. Su Nu decided that she would give the two sessions simultaneously, as both couples were here for similar reasons. She would project her body into two different areas of the garden and give each couple the personal guidance they needed while reducing the wait time for the other students. She always loved to have opportunities to put her thousands of years of cultivation to good use, and this was the perfect time.

As the students sat with her, the teacher introduced the lesson.

"Intimacy is our ability to share great closeness with another. And there are different areas of intimacy that we will want to engage in with our lover. These areas are emotional, sexual, mental, and spiritual intimacy. Intimacy can feel easy and fulfilling as we develop our capacity for sharing in each of these areas. Intimacy can also feel terrifying in those places where we haven't resolved emotional pain. Although intimacy is at times frightening, we can enjoy a richer bond with our loved one when we cultivate intimacy in our relationships."

"Teacher, what if a lover is not able to be intimate in a certain area?" asked one of the female students.

The Immortal replied, "Sacred Lovers choose to invest in relationships where both lovers can share and develop more physical, emotional, mental, and spiritual intimacy rather than bond simply through one connection, such as a sexual or mental connection. If the ability to share intimacy is deficient in either of the individuals, the relationship will be less than fulfilling and can lose its connection. When both lovers' ability to share intimacy is strong, their relationship will offer nourishing and long-lasting benefits to each partner, and the relationship will grow healthier and more pleasing."

One of the male students nervously confessed to the teacher, "I can experience emotional intimacy, but then I reach a point where I feel bored. Is this wrong?"

"Sacred Lovers develop their skill to sustain intimacy," replied Su Nu. "For example, lovers who have not developed their ability for sharing emotional intimacy can enjoy it to a certain point, and then they switch off. This switch-off point is caused by coming in contact with emotional intimate pain. When this personal pain is not faced, it only creates conflict between lovers, and distance and pain within the relationship."

"How can my lover and I develop our ability to sustain intimacy with each other?" asked a female student.

"As Sacred Lovers, you and your partner can develop your ability for intimacy through resolving old emotions that prevent intimacy and by making new choices that will enrich and honor the emotional, physical, mental, and spiritual well-being of yourself and your relationship. It is important that each lover be motivated by a personal desire to become more developed in the ability to share intimacy rather than be motivated solely by external requests from the other lover. As a Sacred Lover cultivates a greater capacity to experience intimacy with their lover, they will create and enjoy a more rewarding intimate relationship."

Talent 1: Intimate Connection

Embracing the fullness of each other can lead our relationships to new vistas of intimate exploration and renewal. By learning to connect with our lover beyond just the body, by sharing heart to heart and soul to soul, we gain greater insights and skills for loving one another into our truest selves and the best relationship possible. Here you will learn to build an intimate connection with Your Sacred Intimate Itinerary and by: Holding the Exalted Space of Love; Claiming the Courage to Love; Learning Relationship Lessons; Committing to Great Love; Taking the Risk: Sharing Heart-to-Heart Intimacy; and Building a Trustworthy Relationship.

Once you've cultivated the lover within yourself, as described in Part One: The Sacred Lover, you are ready to create a passionate, fulfilling intimate connection.

Your intimate connection with your lover is the dance of two hearts, two bodies, and two souls exploring a loving sexual relationship. Your shared similarities and individual differences; your personal intentions, talents, and vulnerabilities; and the ways you each move to the music of relating intimately will determine what your dance will bring forth.

What will your dance of love become?

The driving motivations and themes of your relationship and the opportunities for growth within your coupling will help you discover your dance of love. The talents presented in Part Two will help you navigate, enrich, learn from, and celebrate your own special dance of The Talent of Loving Another.

Your Sacred Intimate Itinerary

When you first recognize that you have established an intimate connection with your Sacred Lover, you experience the elation and joy of feeling that you have come home. Thinking of your partner, being together, and sharing yourself with them can ignite a fire that enlivens your heart, body, and soul. The first moments, days, and months of loving each other are often magical and blissful. You feel you finally understand what life is all about, and you want this feeling to continue.

The inquisitiveness, the excitement, the newness, the passion, the going the extra mile, the great conversations, the love notes, the sweet and sexy whispers all make the intimate connection you share so stimulating and deeply nurturing.

Your dance of love has begun, and you are gliding through the stars.

Discovering the similarities between you and your lover is balm for the soul. The differences can be stimulating, both emotionally and sexually. This is especially relevant when the differences appear in areas that you want to explore and grow in.

Very quickly, you begin to see ideas, themes, motivations, and patterns emerging in your intimate connection. These will determine the sacred path your relationship will take as well as the opportunities that will be provided for you to learn and grow.

What will soon appear are the subjects that you will return to on an ongoing basis—what activities will excite you both and which ones will bore one or the other—what events you will attend and the friends you will make together—the places your connection is harmonious and easy and the places where there is friction and challenge. In other words, you can view your travel itinerary for your Sacred Love relationship early on.

If, overall, your travel itinerary feels disappointing, painful, disrespectful, uncomfortable, or depleting, then it is not the right one for you. In such a case, it is better to stop and reevaluate whether this potential intimate relationship would be better off as a friendship or if it was just a short-term connection that you need to say goodbye to altogether.

But if you feel great and are happy with the travel itinerary, your intimate connection is the right one for you, and you are well on board for great adventures in love, with more magic, romance, and fulfillment to come.

Holding the Exalted Space of Love

Once you have recognized that your path of partnership is the right one for you, it is vital to the success of your relationship to hold the space of recognition for each other. Being able to recognize and be recognized by your lover is a gift that you can offer each other over and over again to awaken the fullest experience of love with one another.

To behold our partners' essence, appreciating them for who they are in totality and what they bring to nurture and love us, is invaluable to supporting their personal best as well as creating a rich, rewarding relationship.

To honor and be honored for your mind, heart, body, and soul in the interactions that you have in your intimate relationship is to be held in an exalted space of love. We can see this positive experience of beholding the other demonstrated in great parenting. A child that is held in love, and supported, and allowed to express their natural authenticity and explore and develop their genuine interests will grow in a direction that is most harmonious and healthy for them. In general, such children are more comfortable and willing to interact with others in a healthy and harmonious way.

Naturally, being loved and supported in our truest authenticity awakens more passion and love in our relationship. For instance, if our partner communicates appreciation and support of a quality that they recognize in us such as our strength, generosity, beauty, or patience, we feel great. This acknowledgement boosts our confidence in that quality and creates more of a desire and ease in expressing it. Another example is if we have a natural talent for playing piano but have yet to fulfill that potential. In this case, if our lover acknowledges our talent and supports us in developing it more fully, we blossom in our newly found self-expression and thus fulfill an unmet part of ourselves.

The following are some of the essential ways you can recognize each other in partnership to enhance your ability to love more fully and be more fully loved in return.

Recognize and Hold the Exalted Space for Your Partner:

- See your partner as a great individual.
- Respect who your partner is authentically without wanting to change the essence of who your partner is or to make him or her more like you.
- Honor and acknowledge your partner's qualities and talents.
- Cherish your partner's body, heart, mind, and soul.

- Hold the vision of your partner's personal empowerment and success even if it doesn't match your own.

- Support your partner in manifesting his or her vision of success.

- Celebrate your partner's life and the love you share.

These acts of sincere respect toward your partner communicate appreciation, love, support, and loyalty. This quality of recognizing and honoring each other is so powerful it can almost instantly create a shared feeling of love, happiness, and even bliss within your relationship.

A true recognition of your partner should be effortless. But often, because of unresolved emotions around love and intimacy and the challenging growth opportunities presented to you in your relationship, you may fail to recognize or admit that you can recognize the greatness of your loved one. For instance, if you have done something very thoughtful for your lover and it is taken for granted, or if you have dressed up especially nice for the day and your lover doesn't say anything, these are both failures of recognition in the relationship.

When you don't recognize what is great in your partner, the tendency is to focus on the opposite, zeroing in on what irritates, frustrates, and concerns you, which lowers your partner's self-esteem, creates conflict, and inhibits connectivity and real intimacy. This can lead the relationship into to a state of stale mediocrity or, even worse, a breakup.

Developing the talent of holding the exalted space of love will build a strong foundation for your love. These are some examples of how to keep the exalted space of love alive in your relationship.

Love Your Partner in an Exalted Way By:

- Verbally appreciating your lover

- Directing a consistent current of love and support to your lover with eye-to-eye contact, hugs, words, and actions

- Playing, growing, having fun, and enthusiastically enjoying your relationship

- Relaxing and being at ease in your love whether you are together or apart

- Being a great emotional support

- Demonstrating emotional commitment and loyalty

When intimate partners recognize and hold the exalted space for each other confidence, love, and both personal *and* relationship success abound.

Claiming the Courage to Love

It takes real courage to love another well. A brave spirit is required to give and receive, share, learn, and keep growing in love. Faced with a variety of challenges, love can be a feat of the emotional fittest.

When we have been hurt or saddened by a love experience it can leave us less than eager to be courageous in this department. Love, though, requires our bravery in order to create the kind of relationship that we really want.

Detaching from the Outcome

Being the first to tell your new partner you are in love, even if you don't know what they will say … Telling your lover the truth about what you want intimately, even though it may be a challenging conversation … These are the moments that define a relationship.

Each of these acts of courage must happen to begin a relationship, bring you and your partner closer, and keep you both growing in your relationship. Detachment from the outcome of the response helps you be courageous in these moments. For instance, you can practice being detached during these acts of courage by acknowledging your worth to yourself and congratulating yourself for taking a new step out of your comfort zone, no matter what the response.

Not that it isn't a bit scary—it is. However, it can also be energizing and exciting to take a risk in love and do what you thought you couldn't. Relinquishing control builds your confidence—even if the answer doesn't go your way—and helps you love with more courage and enthusiasm.

Your Carefree and Joyful Nature

Having lightness in your heart contributes to your courage. Children love naturally and easily. It is always a joy to have a child run up and throw their arms around you and give you a hug and kiss. Connect with your carefree, childlike nature by being more playful and affectionate. These qualities can help you regain your passion, juice, and courage to love with open arms.

Go Ahead

To truly love another, we have to learn to come out of focusing solely on ourselves or focusing solely on our lover and become equally attentive to both. It is our tendency to be absorbed in what only one of us needs and wants, but we can train ourselves to be more sensitive to each other's needs and desires. That way, we can attend to our lover's needs and still not leave ourselves out of the equation.

This is where our courage comes in.

We must be courageous enough to see ourselves and our partner in our fullest joy and divine essence. We must learn to speak our truth and hear our partner's truth, to respect and cherish ourselves and our partner, to support ourselves and our partner in having what we each want in our lives, and to keep sharing and growing in love.

How we consistently apply our courage to love in these areas crystallizes the quality of our relationship. Courage to love another not for a few days, months, or years but for the long term requires ongoing respect, courage, and creativity, abandonment of our need to control, and a real and wondrous connection to our carefree and childlike joy.

Learning Relationship Lessons

All the challenges that we go through in a relationship are there to teach us valuable lessons. These lessons help us discover more about ourselves and how to love another. Sometimes, the particular challenges we face in a relationship feel too hard to bear. The difficulty seems insurmountable, and the easiest thing would be to opt out.

But often, when we do this, we miss the golden opportunity that the lesson presents to us. Lessons are invitations to awaken to our full potential in a relationship. At their core, all lessons can help us become more of who we really are—which is love, integrity, and bliss.

In a healthy, loving relationship, the challenges we are faced with can accelerate our growth exponentially. Lessons may appear in the form of an intimacy challenge, a financial challenge, a family challenge, a logistical challenge, or a health challenge.

It is important to know that there is gold in each of these challenges.

For instance, if your partner has been laid off, and that income is vital to your standard of living, the challenge is not only financial; it will also test your relationship emotionally. If you and your partner can look at the challenge together and open your minds, breathe with the challenge, and think and work creatively through it together, the seeming "obstacles" become manageable, then easier, and then can even disappear.

The challenges that we are presented with are our most needed lessons for individual growth and the development of the relationship. When we recognize this, we can actually feel how every lesson we face loves and caresses us into our most authentic and satisfied selves.

Committing to Great Love

Many years ago, one of my Taoist teachers said before instructing me in a session of Tai Chi, "You must commit in order to win. Without committing yourself one hundred percent, you will not attain what you want." While this wise statement was given to me in preparation for cultivating my Tai Chi practice, it is also the perfect anecdote for achieving great love.

Commitment is fundamental to creating a great relationship. A solid commitment creates a solid relationship. A wavering commitment creates a wavering relationship.

There is always an area of our lives where it has been easy for us to commit. In that area, we see the treasure of our greatest success. Wherever we want to go the distance in our lives requires our generous passion, energy, and dedication. Think of an area in which you have shown this kind of commitment, which in turn has rewarded you with success. Then see it as a model to support you in achieving your commitment to great love.

Commitment is based on honoring the highest qualities that define success: personal integrity, love and passion, generosity, and devotion.

When we make a commitment with these four values, great love manifests in our lives.

Personal Integrity

The first commitment is to yourself to cultivate your own integrity. Again, integrity is the strength of our individual core that is made up of our physical, emotional, mental, and spiritual states. Cultivating our integrity allows us to express ourselves and make choices that are harmonious and fulfilling to our whole self. This commitment also concerns choosing your partner wisely, as we discussed at length in Part One.

Love and Passion

Your second commitment is to love your partner and be passionate about your relationship.

Express ongoing love and passion with your partner. Utilize the tips mentioned in Holding the Exalted Space of Love for reference. If you do not express ongoing love and passion, your relationship can become little more than the sharing of a routine. This may be enough to satisfy you and give you a sense of grounding, belonging, and companionship—but, essentially, a loveless and passionless relationship loses its luster, juice, romance, and all the other reasons you entered it in the first place.

If you have to push yourself out of a routine you have gotten stuck in, do it. Realize that a great relationship is one worth putting your love and passion skills into, to give it life and therefore receive its abundant fruits.

Generosity

Your third commitment is the generosity of time, care, and attention that you offer to your partner and the relationship to make it great.

Become a generous and attentive lover by taking the initiative to find out what matters to your lover. Be mindful of where your lover is emotionally sensitive. Find out what makes your partner respond receptively in love, and passionately during sexual intimacy. Find out what you can give to your relationship to make it healthier and stronger.

A daily habit of generous attention to your partnership can become a powerful ritual, rewarding you with more generous, good feelings and loving experiences.

Devotion

Your fourth commitment is your devotion to giving your loyalty, faithfulness, and dedication to your partnership.

Loyalty, faithfulness, and dedication are demonstrated by bringing all of yourself to this relationship: your body, heart, mind, and spirit are present and available to help this relationship to grow, strengthen, and succeed.

If you have had difficulty with commitment, explore the reasons why. You may have had parents who could not keep their commitments. You may fear being locked into one relationship. You may feel the grass might be greener on the other side and want to keep your options open. Address your reasons in your journal and then, if needed, with a qualified counselor to support you in finding your way to a healthy expression of loyalty and dedication in an intimate relationship.

A fulfilling relationship depends upon both partners' willingness to be active in their commitment on an ongoing basis. When each partner meets the other—not halfway, but one hundred percent—in the relationship, the result is the love that you truly want.

A new couple had come to the garden for a session with the Immortal. As they were waiting for the teacher to arrive, they began arguing. The argument started over the man's emotional shutdown. His lover was beside herself. She had tried being very kind and extra attentive for days, but she had had enough, and she was angry. That was the reason they were here.

"What's wrong?" she asked. "You have been distant and unresponsive to me all week. I feel like I am the only one in this relationship."

Her lover then said, "I need time alone."

"You have said that three times this week," the woman replied, "but nothing changes after your time alone. You still go to bed without saying good night or giving me a kiss, and I'm tired of it."

The man got angry and said, "You don't understand me!"

"What does she need to understand?" asked the Immortal, entering the scene. The couple turned red; they were embarrassed that the teacher had caught them in this unflattering interaction. "Don't feel ashamed," assured the Immortal. "This is why you are here."

The Immortal sat down with the couple and proceeded to listen. After a period of time and some gentle, deep, thought-provoking questioning, the man realized that he had been holding resentment at his partner about something she had said to him during the heat of an argument weeks before, which had painfully affected him. His lover thought that they had moved past the issue, and she was shocked to know that he had not moved on. "I apologize," said the woman to her lover.

The Immortal said to the male student, "You have to be willing to take the risk and share how something affects you when it happens. Otherwise, you can become imprisoned in yourself with those feelings, which will cause your relationship to lose its harmony and cohesiveness. You have been living behind a wall of protection the last few weeks that may have felt safe but ultimately was lonely and low on love. Only when you open your heart again to the relationship can your issue be resolved and your relationship begin moving in a positive, loving direction."

The male student bowed thankfully to the teacher. His lover joined him.

Taking the Risk: Sharing Heart-to-Heart Intimacy

If you love someone, shouldn't it be the most natural of experiences to share emotionally with that person?

Initially, sharing emotional intimacy with a new person can be easy. We can feel the joy and freedom of easily expressing our feelings, appreciation, ideas, innermost thoughts, and our secrets. In that initial period of sharing intimacy, we feel alive, free, and even more in love.

However, the more time we spend in the relationship, a tendency to share less emotional intimacy begins to set in. Why is that?

Because sharing our heart now becomes riskier.

The deeper our connection becomes with another, the more likely it is that sharing emotional intimacy can bring up our vulnerability. It can also bring up fear that we will not be loved when we really expose ourselves. In addition, emotional intimacy can threaten our sense of individual ego and our feeling of security in the relationship. When this happens, we tend to feel protective of ourselves and want to control our connection to our partner. One of the ways that this pattern shows up is in how we share or do not share emotional intimacy.

Emotionally Open and Emotionally Closed Off

We have one of two choices when our fears arise about exposing ourselves and sharing emotional intimacy. The first is to remain emotionally open, and the second is to close down emotionally.

Being emotionally open and intimate may or may not feel natural to you. You may take your vulnerabilities, fears, and frustrations in stride and still keep showing up and being emotionally present in love. If that is true, congratulations—you are on the path to a very successful relationship! You have realized that by connecting to the river of love and not shutting off from it, you will actually enjoy it and have more of it.

But for most people, staying open and emotionally intimate in a relationship is a talent that generally takes maturity and great attention.

You have probably found yourself in a situation where you emotionally stop connecting as strongly as you once did. You may not even recall how this pattern started. Perhaps you have projected the reason onto your partner: your partner doesn't or cannot hear you or give you what you need, or your partner is not making you happy. Likewise, you may have projected the reason onto yourself: now that you have the relationship you want, you don't feel good enough, you are always getting it wrong, or you want more individual space.

Assuming that you have chosen a partner with whom you truly connected in the beginning, then it is your pulling back and closing off from the flow of love that is creating the lack of fulfillment and rich interactions that you crave.

When you feel emotionally hurt by your partner or your partnership triggers an old emotional memory, there is a natural inclination to retreat. For instance, if your partner made you feel inferior by dismissing your opinion in front of others, you could shut down. That's because being emotionally hurt does not foster a desire to be open, and in intimate relationships there are times where we hurt each other emotionally.

It is important to be aware of the emotional pain that you are experiencing and how often it is occurring. Your emotions are indicators of what is healthy for you and what isn't. So the tendency to shut down when you are hurt can inform you whether the dynamic of your intimate relationship is healthy or unhealthy. By noting where you are experiencing emotional shutdown, you can gain greater clarity about what you need for greater health and well-being within your relationship.

While the tendency to withdraw when you have experienced hurt makes you feel safer, you have to be careful that the situation doesn't shut you down for a long time or completely. Opening back up as soon as possible is important to starting the river of love flowing again, bringing forth joy, love, and fulfilling intimacy in your relationship.

Opening Up After Emotional Shutdown

Mild Shutdown, During or After an Argument

Situation: You are having or have had an argument with your lover, and you feel angry, misunderstood, and hurt. The argument has not been resolved, and the problem is left hanging. These are the moments that can cause you to shut down emotionally, retreat, leave the room, or go silent for moments, hours, or longer.

When you feel angry and hurt, it is easy to want to retaliate and be hurtful toward the other or disengage emotionally, but that will never resolve your feelings of pain; it will only perpetuate them.

Opening Up from Mild Shutdown

If you feel compelled to shut down in the middle of an argument or after an unresolved argument, try these steps instead:

Option One

- Take a moment to allow the intensity of your feelings to subside.

Option Two

- If this will take you more than a moment or two, communicate in the most even tone possible that you need to take some time before you will be able to communicate your feelings in a healthy way.

Option Three

- If you are enraged by a point or criticism that your partner has made and want to shut down or leave the room, stop and breathe deeply in and out three times. Relax and stay present.

Utilize the next steps with any of the above options:

- Once you have come back to a feeling of balance, communicate your feelings calmly. For instance, discuss what has made you want to shut down or leave the room and why. (Usually the shutdown plays on your emotions of not feeling good enough.)
- Communicate with the intention of resolving the issue and staying open to love.

Moderate Shutdown, After a Series of Disagreements Over the Same Issue

Arguing repeatedly about the same problem without the issue improving or resolving itself can cause you to feel a sense of futility and can create a dull, aching pain that permeates your relationship.

Perpetual arguments over the same issue can shut down your emotional connection with your partner, causing you to hold onto your hurt or anger and disengage from the relationship for longer periods of time. You can lose interest in initiating intimate interaction for extended periods, thus moving through the day-to-day experience of the relationship wanting to avoid confrontation.

Opening Up from Moderate Shutdown

If you are moderately shut down, take action with these steps:

- Be willing to let go of your hurt, anger, and resentment toward your partner.
- Be willing to let go of the issue altogether and not bring it up again.
- Appoint a time to resolve the issue together. Don't end the communication period until you have come up with an amicable solution.
- Seek the help of a qualified counselor to help you through a difficult issue if you and your partner cannot resolve it yourselves.

Experiencing Extreme Shutdown from the Experience of Emotional or Physical Betrayal

If you have been emotionally or physically betrayed by your partner from being lied to, cheated on, or abused, it is extremely difficult to stay open to your partnership—and in many cases it is not appropriate to do so.

It is important to retreat from an emotionally or physically abusive relationship in order to assess the seriousness of the situation. Often, when we are being betrayed or are involved in an abusive relationship, we feel pain, distress, and illness, and we lose interest in sexual interaction but cannot get clarity on what is going on. Shutting down from intimate interaction in the relationship can be a healthy reaction to an unhealthy situation. It is important to listen to your inner voice and the signals it gives you.

When you have clearly identified that you have been betrayed—through confronting the issue with your partner or finding out the facts another way—then you must deal with the situation. If you do not deal with it, the betrayal can destroy your health and well-being. In addition, if you decide to leave the relationship without dealing with the issue, it can appear again in a new relationship.

Opening up from Extreme Shutdown in Situations of Betrayal

If you are experiencing extreme shut down, take action with these steps:

- Salvaging a relationship depends totally on *both* people doing the work it takes to get to the root of the issue and regain trust.

- Building trust once it has been destroyed is a difficult feat that usually takes a long period of time, but it is possible if both partners are committed to taking positive, consistent action to build a healthy relationship. Only then is openness in a betrayed relationship a wise choice.

- Whether or not you stay in the relationship, I recommend seeing a qualified counselor to help you through the layers of emotions that are the byproduct of betrayal.

- If you have decided to leave the relationship, it is important to also work with a skilled counselor to help you resolve your personal issues of why you attracted the betrayal and how you can prevent it again. This will help you feel confident in opening yourself up to an intimate relationship in the future.

Being emotionally open and able to share yourself in intimacy offers you the freedom of being authentic. You are rewarded by discovering more about yourself and your partnership and by the renewal found in creating a deeper love. The more skilled you become, the more you will find that you will close off less and for shorter periods of time, until you ultimately decide you don't need to close off to emotional intimacy at all. It is always your choice.

Building a Trustworthy Relationship

Most of us have been touched by the hurt of betrayal or abandonment in intimate relationships, whether by a parent, lover, friend, or spouse. These experiences can make us feel pessimistic about love and fearful of whether anyone can be trusted.

Without trust as the foundation of a relationship, there can be no real mutually nurturing and evolving love. As soon as one partner stops being trustworthy, the relationship—whether or not the other partner is aware of it—loses its underlying stability, which in turn halts the relationship's ability to grow and succeed. Only when trustworthiness is reestablished does the relationship begin to thrive again.

Rest assured, trustworthy relationships *do* exist, and in them we find both individuals and the relationship thrive. But how do we create a trusting intimate relationship, especially if we've been hurt by our current partner or a previous partner?

Building a trustworthy relationship first requires that you trust yourself. The act of trusting yourself leads to building a trusting relationship. Let's find out the kind of trust you have for yourself in a relationship.

On a scale of one to ten, with ten being the highest, how much do you trust yourself to make the right decisions in these areas?

	1-10
Physically	_____
Sexually	_____
Emotionally	_____
Intellectually	_____
Career/life path	_____

Do your words and actions match the level of trust that you have noted for yourself?

Do the rewards you receive in these areas of your life and your relationship match the level of trust you have written down?

Are you more fulfilled in your relationship in the areas where you have given yourself higher marks?

The more we trust ourselves, the more we create trustworthiness. A partner we can trust is a manifestation of our capacity to value and trust our own worth. A partner we can trust will also be someone who will encourage our self-worth and empowerment, which, in turn, will support a more trusting love relationship. However, the areas where we do not value and trust our own worth will cause us to draw into our lives experiences that do not show us our worth. This is to teach us to value ourselves and develop trust in these specific areas.

Act with Integrity

If you seek a trustworthy intimate relationship, be the person you wish to be in a relationship with. Always speak honestly, keep your word, and act with integrity toward yourself, the person you love, and other people.

It is important to nourish ourselves with self-love, exercise, and spiritual wisdom and also with healthy foods, thoughts, and activities. If we do not fill ourselves with real nourishment—both emotionally and physically—we come to a relationship from a place of emptiness. Emptiness produces wanting and neediness, which creates a variety of behaviors that push away a truly loving, trusting, healthy relationship.

Take care of yourself so that your inner being is harmonious and whole.

Discernment

Seeing clearly what is right in front of us is an important skill for creating an intimate relationship that we can trust.

Many of us have found ourselves falling into the well-intentioned pitfall of seeing the potential in someone. Our projections of what someone might become, however, can leave us living in the hope of the future and with the illusions of what "might be," instead of trusting what is present right now.

People are capable of amazing feats of change, especially when they are committed to self-reflection and growth. However, awareness and discernment of what values, strengths, patterns, pursuits, and actions are present within a person in the present moment will more accurately define who that person is now and will become later. By taking a thorough look at what is right in front of us, we can more effectively gauge the trustworthiness of a person now.

Roots of Betrayal

The roots of betrayal are based in the betrayal of ourselves.

When we rush into partnership without getting to know if a person is really right for us, we betray ourselves. When we are not honest with ourselves about what our real needs are for love and do not communicate them truthfully with our partner, then these needs live in the shadows of our psyche, acting out in unconscious ways, and we betray ourselves.

If we have betrayed ourselves, our partner gets the backlash of that betrayal, and we project onto the partner what is wrong with the relationship. Affairs are acted out in search of what we feel is lacking in our relationship.

If you have been a betrayer, take a look at how you betrayed yourself and projected that unhappiness onto your partner and your relationship. If you have been betrayed, take a look at how you did not honor and respect yourself, and how you did not stay committed to yourself in your life and in the relationship, thereby bringing on the betrayal.

Reasons That a Lover Will Betray a Partner:

- Denying a part of oneself that is mandatory to one's well-being
- Not feeling seen or understood
- Not feeling cherished and loved
- Being fearful of asking for one's partnership needs to be met
- Being unable to share stress and responsibilities
- Not experiencing a connection emotionally, sexually, mentally, and/or spiritually
- Experiencing low self-worth
- Engaging in addictive behavior
- Feeling boredom or feeling that the passion and excitement of the relationship is dead

Coming out of a pattern of betrayal requires claiming the courage to be honest with yourself about what you need and, in your communications, and your actions with your partner.

By confronting your feelings of betrayal with honesty and clarity, you will find yourself on the edge of a more passionate, healthier relationship and real, intimate love.

Overcoming Hurt

If you have been hurt by an untrustworthy partner, it is hard to want to trust again or to fully commit to being trustworthy yourself. Be willing to break the cycle. Continuing it just creates a pattern of disharmony and untrustworthiness in your life.

Even though it may be challenging, create a trustworthy identity through your words and actions that will develop more trust in yourself and draw more trust into your life.

Surround Yourself with Trustworthy People

Create a support system of trustworthy people who will help you cultivate better discernment in order to develop a trustworthy intimate relationship.

Building trust within ourselves and our lives allows us the ability to create the safety and confidence that we deeply want and need in a healthy, loving relationship. As we settle into a foundation of trust, we can more easily open our hearts, relax our bodies, and share our dreams to our greatest ability with a partner truly worthy of our trust.

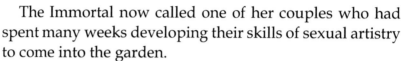

The Immortal now called one of her couples who had spent many weeks developing their skills of sexual artistry to come into the garden.

When the couple arrived, the Immortal tuned in to their energy fields to assess their development. "You are ready to learn how to utilize your sexual artistry as sexual alchemists," announced the Immortal, looking pleased.

This excited both lovers. "Thank you, teacher," they responded.

"You have begun to glimpse the great creative power of sex. Have you not?" asked the Immortal.

"Yes," they replied.

"Sexual alchemists possess not only the awareness of sexual power, but they can respectfully harness this power to make a sacred tonic for regeneration, creative brilliance, and lasting intimate fulfillment together.

"Sexual alchemy will provide the cauldron for your sexual artistry, whereby you can richly brew it and use it to benefit your relationship." The Immortal then vaporized. A green cauldron filled with steaming, sweet-and-spiced-scented tea was left in her place.

Two cups appeared in the lovers' hands. The Immortal's voice was heard saying, "Drink and meditate on this alchemical stage of your lovers journey together."

Talent 2: Sexual Alchemy

It is time to discover the ancient Taoist knowledge of sex as alchemy, a unique process of sharing, healing, and transformation, for your relationship. You will be introduced to the unique opportunities available through sex to love another artfully and produce empowering, creative, healthy, and bliss-filled rewards. These opportunities include: Becoming a Sexual Alchemist, Awakening and Healing the Body, Co-Creativity, Cultivating Sexual Respect, and Enjoying a Deeper Relationship with Sexual Pleasure.

Becoming a Sexual Alchemist

Sex brings peace or misery according to our degree and understanding of it and application of it.
    —Napoleon Hill

It is important to recognize the powerful wand that we hold in our hands when we interact sexually.

Sexual chemistry is a source of incredible power and alchemy. We have all felt the hypnotic power of sexual chemistry drawing us toward a person we have wanted to become our lover. If we have become lovers, we have felt the joy and pleasure of sexually bonding with this person, and this connection may have lasted long after the sexual act took place—for hours or even days.

The power of our sexual chemistry with another arises out of feelings of aliveness and pleasure that are beyond any other human experience. Our ability to create life as well as deepen the bond of a relationship are the vital gifts of our sexual chemistry. And if we allow it, sexual chemistry can also connect us to some of the deepest possible experiences we can share physically, emotionally, and spiritually with another.

The ancient Taoists understood the powerful alchemy available in sexual chemistry. Sex was revered by the Taoist love masters for its potential to bond, create, and heal. They noticed that, like with any power, how we choose to utilize sex would determine a positive or negative outcome. Free of sexual judgments, the Taoists developed the talent of sexual alchemy as a means of cultivating and utilizing the sexual essence to benefit the individual and deepen love between two partners. This process could strengthen the nucleus of the family as a whole.

The Jing Zing

From the Taoist perspective, the sexual chemistry we share with our lover is connected to our Jing essence. Jing, which originates in the kidneys, is the quality of our physical vitality and life force. The zing that you feel when you share sexual chemistry with your lover is a result of you having complementary Jing essences. The more complementary your Jings are, the more sensational the zing. The Jing governs sexual response, physical regeneration, and the creative impulse.

Besides the kidneys and reproductive organs, our Jing is related to another area of the physical body: our bone marrow. The bone marrow is the storehouse of millions of our blood cells, which contain all kinds of deeply personal information. Therefore, when we have sex, we are actually communicating with our lover on a cellular level. We make an agreement, most likely unconsciously, to share our deepest information. The information we receive from our lover is processed in our cells, and vice versa, the information they receive from us is processed in their cells. It's like downloading a new program into our computer hard drive.

This super-cellular-bonding effect of sex can be hypnotizing and can feel very moving and powerful. A woman or man can fall in love or feel bonded to someone before a sexual experience, but the Jing can heighten this effect after a sexual experience. When we understand this inherent power of sex, we possess the alchemist key to open the door to the greater meaning of sex and its benefits for long-lasting health and well-being.

The proper utilization of our Jing can offer profound benefits to an intimate relationship. Our shared Jing chemistry can compose an awakening and healing for our bodies, unity for our hearts, and an ecstatic symphony for our spirits.

On the next several pages, you will discover intriguing ways to create sexual alchemy through the respectful use of your sexual expression.

Awakening and Healing the Body

The sexual chemistry we share is a great reservoir of energy that can be tapped into to bring us more overall regeneration and vitality. Learning to cultivate our sexual energy with the arts described in Part One, Sex as Sacred Artistry, and Part Three, The Art of Sacred Love-Making, will help us generate more sexual energy and channel it through our and our lover's bodies. These arts will allow us to exchange sexual energy with our lover in the act of lovemaking, strengthening our immune system, and restoring health and wholeness.

Understanding proper management for our sexual energy is important. If sex is utilized recklessly without respect for our emotional or physical health, or without having an emotional connection with our lover, sex can deplete our Jing. In addition, if sex is utilized to cause pain, then we are misusing our sexual energy. Misusing sexual energy is destructive; it causes fragmentation between the body and mind of the individuals who participate, which can create harmful physical and emotional repercussions.

On the other hand, having sex when we feel emotionally harmonious and rested and we want to share love, pleasure, and intimacy with our lover can restore health, well-being, and vitality. It can actually nourish our cells and our minds. There are times when we may even desire to schedule sex for the purpose of healing and restoring ourselves, through gentle, slow, or precise movements (described in Part Three: The Art of Sacred Love-Making). Emotionally harmonious sexual sharing can greatly support our physical health—we can observe this in a lover's healthy afterglow.

The Afterglow

Everyone who has made love in an emotionally harmonious exchange has most likely experienced the radiant afterglow of sex. Have you ever wondered why you emanate a glow of health and vitality after great sex? As you have just discovered, it is because you actually do become healthier. One of the great by-products of a healthy sexual exchange is the appearance of vibrancy.

The Taoists believe that every time we have sex, we have the ability to rejuvenate ourselves, exhibiting a more youthful body and appearance. This rejuvenation process works in the following way: As we make love, sexual energy moves from our pelvic region toward our vital organs and filters into the various systems of the body. Then each organ and system sends vital energy to an outer part of our body, like the skin, ears, eyes, mouth, and so forth. This is one of the deeper reasons why we crave sexual contact: we actually know it's inherently good for us and will make us feel and look great!

Co-Creativity

Creativity is the river and juice of our lives. Wit.
wooden and mechanical.

Sexual energy activates our creative juices: a woman .
man's semen and sweat. These juices are representative of .
ened when we have sex and when we feel pleasure.

Are your creative juices aroused in your life and relationship?

If not, what pleasure will bring forth your waters?

Within a loving, intimate relationship, co-creation becomes a wonde..
adventures.

The Taoist teachings of the Art of Love regard our creative energy as inc.
and sexual. Although we utilize all of ourselves to create—including our heart,
and imagination—it is sexual energy that is most known for its creative and life-g..
ers. Rising up from our sexual center, creativity springs forth, expressing itself in a var.
desired creative ways. If two lovers give their attention, love, and vitality to a creative proce
like in the act of lovemaking, a juicy creation of any kind can take form.

Developing our awareness of and cultivating our sexual essence can free our creativity. This
creativity can unfold within us by harnessing the incredible power inherent in our sexuality to
create life. We can choose to utilize our creative energy both individually and with our lover to
take many forms of creative genius: love, play, art, healing, or anything else we wish. Bringing
our creative inspiration to our intimate relationships can generate more excitement and many
valuable, co-creative experiences.

Creative Responsibility

Our creative power carries great responsibility. It is important to use it positively and benefi-
cially for ourselves and others.

Ways to Use Your Creativity Positively:

- Bringing forth a loved and wanted human life
- Co-creating business or community projects
- Manifesting dreams
- Developing new skills or interests

ut these waters, we dry up and become

exual secretions and breast milk, a

creative aliveness that is awak-

exciting current of

ly arousing
ds, mind,
pow-
of

atively, it becomes destructive

substance or with a depleted

ility to love, nurture, and take

rson or situation

• Solely focusing on what is wrong with our partner and what isn't going right with our relationship. This can turn our creative power into a destructive force that cuts away at our relationship and the love we share

Be mindful of all the ways that you are co-creating in your relationship. With your partner, review where you are directing your creativity on a regular basis and notice the results of those pursuits. The more aware you are of how you are currently creating, the more you can focus on utilizing your sexual chemistry in your relationship to create the alchemy of health, love, and sexual fulfillment. This is key to both your personal and relationship wellbeing.

Write in your journal about how you are using your creativity positively. In what areas are you using your creativity negatively?

Cultivating Sexual Respect

Sexual health issues have surfaced across the globe. Sexual discord appears in men and women regardless of country, race, sexual orientation, nationality, or age group. Infertility, impotence, child abuse, and AIDS are epidemics that have shocked us into becoming aware of the critical sexual and reproductive malaise happening all around us.

These issues demand that we reflect, respect, and take responsibility for our personal sexual health and the sexual health of those we share sexual intimacy with.

Respect for and within sexual intimate activity is the foundation of cultivating the sexual talent of loving another. Acting with respectfulness and safety gives us the freedom to experience not only sexual health but also the fullest benefits of sacred sex.

Sacred Lovers know that sexual decisions can have lasting effects on their overall health and quality of life. Sacred Lovers make choices about sexual interactions only after thoughtful consideration. They honor their integrity in sharing themselves with another. The talent of sexual respect supports a Sacred Lover's emotional and sexual well-being as well as his or her partner's.

Talent of Safe Sex

By utilizing mindfulness in your sexual relationship, you will create an atmosphere of trust that nurtures each partner's physical health and emotional well-being.

Prepare consciously with your partner prior to engaging in a sexual relationship by having an honest discussion with your potential intimate partner about your sexual health concerning STDs (sexually transmitted diseases) and HIV status. Utilize a condom for intercourse and oral sex if you do not know the sexual health status of a partner or are not having a monogamous relationship. Have an AIDS test with your intimate partner prior to having sex without a condom. Stay up to date on measures to prevent contracting or spreading STDs, especially if one partner already has an STD. And, if you are heterosexual, agree on a method of birth control that works for both you and your partner.

Talent of Sexual Mindfulness

Sexual energy is creative, and when you are around someone you find attractive, your sexual energy can move out toward that person without you even being aware of it. This scenario can be transformed into a wonderful experience by becoming mindful of the movement of your sexual energy, or it may snowball into an unhealthy or unfulfilling sexual interaction if you are not aware of how to manage your sexual energy.

Becoming conscious of how your sexual energy travels can be very empowering. This talent can help you make the connections you really want and can curtail sexual misconceptions and unwanted connections.

Practice the Talent of Sexual Mindfulness

When you are with a special someone or lover that you have sexual chemistry with and *it is appropriate and desirable* for both of you to pursue the connection:

- Become aware of your sexual energy as a vibration that can be directed.
- Enjoy playing and experimenting in the field of your sexual vibrations together.
- Without even touching, you can experience the pleasure and strength of your sexual connection by acknowledging your sexual chemical vibrations.

On the other hand, have you ever found your sexual energy leading you into undesirable circumstances? Perhaps your sexual energy has sent out a strong sexual signal to someone you were attracted to, but it led you down a road that was not optimal for you or the other person. Some examples of this experience could be: if you only had a sexual connection with the person and nothing else in common, if you were in a business relationship and your sexual connection led to compromised business relations, or if you are already in an intimate committed relationship, and connecting with someone else sexually would create betrayal or other unwanted results.

When you are with someone you find you have sexual chemistry with but *it is not appropriate* to share sexual energy:

- Tune into your sexual vibration.
- Instead of directing your sexual vibration toward the other person, redirect it so that it travels down your pelvis, through your legs, into the ground, and then back up from the pelvis through your torso, arms, neck, head, and upwards. This redirection of your sexual energy can offer you great nourishment through invigoration and vitality.

It is important not to shut down your sexual energy but instead to acknowledge it and let it move through your body easily and joyously to nourish and energize you. At the same time, this talent of redirection can spare you and the other person from sexual discomfort, misconceptions, and haphazard reactions. This talent will help to support you in creating healthy, energetic sexual interactions with others.

Enjoying a Deeper Relationship with Sexual Pleasure

We can co-create a deeper, more ecstatic relationship through enjoying our sexuality with our partner. Sex can excite, enliven, and pleasure our bodies. Sex can also open our hearts and expand our spirits. Sharing healthy sexuality with our lover regularly creates more harmony, wholeness, and love within our relationship.

As we learn to open up more to each other during sexual intimacy, we can experience even more pleasure and ecstasy. By connecting and expressing our sexuality with our whole body, heart, mind, and spirit, sex becomes a sacred and unifying experience. This increased opening of ourselves to each other during sexual intimacy is the art of sacred sexuality. This kind of sexual interaction can fill our mind and body with sensations of pleasure. It can also transcend both our mind and body to connect us with the feeling of deep oneness with our lover, nature, and the universe.

Without confidence and ease in our ability to share emotional openness and sexual openness—as detailed in Part One: The Sacred Lover—it is likely that physically or emotionally disconnected sex has been or is currently part of our intimate experience. In this case, sex may feel like a chore, and it may even be difficult to get sexually aroused within our relationship. If so, we can develop a tendency to rely on exterior stimulants such as fantasy, pornography, intoxicating substances, high-risk situations, or pain in order to have a stimulating and fulfilling sexual experience.

The challenge and the opportunity when this happens is to cultivate our openness to share more of ourselves in sexual intimacy. To begin the process, refer to Part One. When we take the steps detailed there to open more fully to sexual intimacy, we begin to have a more exciting and sacred sexual experience. This quality of sexual sharing gives us the emotional connection, sensational pleasure, and even the spiritual fulfillment that are quintessential to having the sexual satisfaction we want and the relationship wholeness we seek.

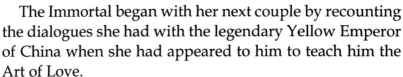

The Immortal began with her next couple by recounting the dialogues she had with the legendary Yellow Emperor of China when she had appeared to him to teach him the Art of Love.

"Once, a very long time ago during one of my visits to the Yellow Emperor, he asked me, 'While my sexual technique is correct, why do I feel minimal satisfaction with my lover?'

"At the time, I replied, "Simply focusing on sexual technique as the key to your intimate fulfillment is keeping you on the surface of intimacy. That may seem safe to a vulnerable heart, but it only protects you from your real capacity to be nourished and moved by love. While it is challenging, like climbing to the top of the Sacred Tao Mountains, Wu Dang, the reward of loving another fully is a sweet, suffusing, intimate satisfaction for two.'"

The Immortal could see some discomfort on her students' faces as she told them the story. She knew that this was a challenging area for their relationship.

Su Nu continued. "Love your partner by developing your talents of expression. Your expressions must be more artful, meaningful, truthful and real.

"With more developed expression, you can enjoy deeper pleasure and even more intimate union with one another in the bedroom and beyond the bedroom. In a stimulating, authentic, and respectful communicative environment, each partner can open their heart, mind and body more fully to experience a greater connection and more satisfaction in each moment of intimacy."

Talent 3: Loving Communication

Great communication holds powerful magic for your relationship. The cultivation of loving expression is an important—yet often overlooked—prerequisite to the sharing and deepening of love. Learning to express your love and intimate thoughts are keys to supporting and nurturing a healthy, harmonious, sexy, passionate relationship. The Talents of Communication you will learn here include: Expressing Love Poetry; Affection; Communicating Active Love; Speaking the Truth; Sexy Communication; Listening; Communication During Conflict; Overcoming the Communications of Demand, Criticism, and Control; The Talking Stick Ritual; and Silent Communication.

Expressing Love Poetry

Throughout history, great poets such as Rumi, Shakespeare, and Rilke have sought to communicate the words, feelings, and experiences of love. These love poets show us the kindredness of our love experiences and inspire our hearts to even greater love. Like poetry, expressing our love to each other in relationship is a talent. The presence of expressing our love can bring our lover closer, and the absence of expressing our love can move us apart. With everything that we say and do, or do not say and do, in intimate relationships we communicate about our feelings of love. We are expressing our priorities, our emotions, and our happiness or unhappiness.

The demands, stresses, and challenges of everyday life can disrupt a partnership and can make it challenging to communicate lovingly. However, starting the flow of loving communication in our relationship can help dissolve stress, create more meaning in the relationship, resolve long-held issues, and create more connectivity with our loved one.

In this chapter, we will explore communications of love—in essence, our "love poetry" of affection, action, truth, listening, and silence—and how to become a more skillful love artist in these areas. We each need these different types of loving communication, and, at the same time, we gravitate to the forms of communication that are easiest for us to express.

While partners can differ in what form of communication is easiest for them, each partner can be deeply fed by cultivating a variety of loving communications and by exchanging them with each other. Through healthy shared communication in an intimate relationship, partners can let go of their emotional walls and unite their energies for sacred intimacy.

Loving Communication

It is always vital to keep the flow of loving communication in your relationship alive. Just the simple act of letting your lover know you love them, or conveying the positive thoughts or feelings you are having for your lover that day, can build a strong foundation of emotional harmony and support a positive, shared energy between the two of you. Communicating lovingly on a daily basis will filter into other positive interactions with your family, friends, and coworkers.

Expand your repertoire of daily loving communication with the following examples to enjoy a more loving partnership:

- Speak the positive feelings you have in your heart for your lover.
- Tell your partner "I love you" often.

- Communicate the reasons why your partner is special to you.
- Verbalize positive support of your partner's self-expression.
- Express your appreciation for the things your partner does for you.
- Communicate support to your lover when he or she is going through a difficult time.

Affection

Showing affection through touch is an essential need of every human being and a wonderful way to communicate love to another. Touch is great for our mental, emotional, and physical well-being, and daily doses of affection shared in this way with our loved one enrich our relationship's connectivity.

Affection is considered a Yin style of communication generally associated with feminine expression. This is why women may naturally gravitate to expressing love this way. Each of us has Yin, a feminine nature, and Yang, a masculine nature, within us. So for lovers who find it more challenging to express affection through touch, this talent is an opportunity to soften and cultivate more of their Yin nature.

Give your loved one daily nurturing doses of affection in these ways:

- Hugs
- Kisses
- Holding Hands
- Cuddling
- Sensual Touch and Massage
- Making Love

Communicating Active Love

Actions speak loudly of your love for one another. Take action in ways that will tell your loved one that you really care. Active love is considered a Yang style of communication generally associated with the masculine. Here are some ways you can express Yang love to your partner to bring out your positive Yang nature.

Love Actions:

- Do something for your lover that he or she asked you to do or mentioned that he or she would like to have done.

- Surprise your lover by doing something they would normally do for you.

- Help your loved one in pursuing their dreams and aspirations.

- Initiate and share responsibilities that need to be taken care of in your relationship together—for instance, household chores, financial responsibilities, child rearing, pet care, and social planning duties. This love action can help you create an even healthier intimate relationship of equality.

Speaking the Truth

It can be challenging to communicate true feelings. We usually believe that communicating our truth will lead to making ourselves vulnerable, hurting our partner, creating an argument, or even breaking up. When any of these beliefs are in place, communication of truthful feelings often comes out in anger, blame, or grief.

However, learning that you can express important feelings and truthfulness and communicate them in a healthy way can lead to becoming a more authentic person and a more present and responsive partner. Sharing honest feelings with one another creates clarity and strengthens trust between you and your partner. Communicating honestly can also develop greater understanding for each other, healing for both of you, and a vibrant relationship dynamic.

Communicating Truthfulness:

- Relax your body and breathe deeply.
- Trust your ability to communicate your feelings calmly and responsibly.
- Be considerate and sensitive to your partner as you communicate.
- Focus on communicating that this is the way you *feel* about a specific situation, rather than conveying something like, "You did this and this to me."
- Don't let issues build. Communicate your feelings in a timely manner—within a day or two of the feeling arising.
- Communicate at an appropriate moment, allowing both the time and place for a healthy conversation to take place.

Generally, we are receptive to truth when it is presented in a way that is respectful to us. You will always get a much more receptive response when you take the above steps.

Asking for What You Want Sexually

Some of us have a hard time asking for what we need and want sexually, because we think that asking will hurt our lover's feelings or that our lover simply will not be able to give us what we need. But asking our lover for what we want, with tenderness and respect, can actually clear up uncertainty for our partner and show them new ways of interacting and experiencing pleasure with us. Rather than feeling bad or resentful about not having what we really want sexually, here are some things you can do.

Steps for Asking for What You Want Sexually:

- Make sure you are in a private space and have the time to communicate. It could be in bed prior to having sex or in another room of the house at another time.

- For certain things, such as conveying how a certain touch or position feels or is affecting you, it is appropriate to communicate in the moment. But more sensitive issues, like asking for your lover to become more giving or discussing the desire to prolong lovemaking, should be addressed prior to sex and preferably outside of the bedroom.

- Open up and share your feelings about your sex life.

- Tell your lover what you need, such as what positions, angles, sensitivity, connection, or points of pleasure will give you greater satisfaction.

- Communicate about what you want without making your lover feel he or she is wrong.

- Don't be afraid to show and tell your lover exactly what you mean.

- Explore Part Three: The Art of Sacred Love-Making together to widen your repertoire for lovemaking.

- Make a commitment to co-create more fulfilling sexual intimacy with each other.

Sexy Communication

When we are leading up to sexual intimacy, or are in the throes of sexual passion, it is emotionally fulfilling to hear and express our arousal, our immediate visceral feelings, and how much our partner means to us. Sharing sexy, honest feelings with one another creates a sensual mood between us and our partner.

It is important to stay away from derogative and demeaning names, words, and phrases. They can lower our partner's self-esteem and hinder the connection within our relationship.

Sexy Things to Say:

- Tell your lover how sexy, hot, handsome, or beautiful he or she is.

- Express how you really feel with phrases like "I love you." "You are amazing." "You turn me on." "I want to be with you."

- Utilize other positive words or questions to arouse sensual touch and affection, honor your partner, turn the heat up, and deepen your emotional connection. For example, "I want to devour you." "That feels so great." "Yes!" "You're the best." "How does this feel?" "Does this arouse you?"

Listening

Great listening is a fine art. When we sit in active, interested silence and open our heart and mind to listening to our intimate partner, we create an inviting environment for truth and transformation to occur. Holding the space for our partner to speak truthfully helps the communicator feel acknowledged, supported, and understood.

It is not necessary for the listener to agree with what the partner is saying, but it is necessary to show love and respect during the communication period. The listener is the witness who observes and takes in the truth of the other. To develop your skill as a listener, sink into a deeper awareness of your partner. This alone can help the other to be fully heard, which can bring clarity and lightness to your partnership. While some communicators appreciate hearing respectful suggestions when they are speaking, others do not. A master skill of listening is learning to listen to your loved one without interruption.

Steps for Listening in Love:

- Sit quietly and open yourself up to receive the communication of your lover.
- Allow the communication to move through you.
- Listen to your partner with respect, empathy, and mindfulness.
- Take in what your partner is communicating.
- Don't interrupt.
- If what your lover is saying brings up feelings of low self-esteem, fear, anger, or wanting to leave the room, acknowledge them to yourself silently and tell your partner about them at the appropriate time.
- Acknowledge your lover's communicated feelings with love by saying, "I hear you" after your lover has finished. Or repeat back what your lover has said, taking it in even more fully.
- Sit for a minute or two, digesting what has been said, before communicating your own feelings about what your lover has said.
- Then it is your turn to communicate and your lover's turn to listen attentively to you in the same manner.

Communication During Conflict

Communication can make or break a relationship in times of conflict. For instance, if we communicate consciously and sensitively during conflict, we foster more health and love in the relationship. If we scream and yell and act aggressively or threaten the other during conflict, we foster an unhealthy relationship.

Choose communication during these challenging times that will make your relationship more honest, close, and strong. This communication may require several of the talents of communication at once, such as listening and speaking truthfully.

First, Don't Let Things Go Unsaid

Address issues when they come up, or they can escalate and become bigger problems. Most conflicts begin between two people because of their different styles of addressing tasks and issues. Arguments also arise in relationships due to a person's inability to communicate effectively to their partner and act respectfully toward them. The best way to resolve a problem that arises in a relationship is through clear, honest, respectful communication. Give your union the time it needs for sharing deeper communication. Issues can bring new awareness and growth to a relationship. Allow the issues that challenge you to lead you to greater personal understanding and fulfillment with one another. When issues arise, discuss them in a loving and timely way to move into an even greater level of intimacy.

Second, Remember: Communication During Conflict Can Bring Up the Feeling of "I'm Not Good Enough"

Listening to our partner's feelings of frustration and disappointment in the relationship can bring up painful, fearful, and angry feelings of not being good enough or not being able to do things right, or feelings that we are being made wrong or are being unfairly judged.

This pain is usually what turns a communication into an argument. Our pain sparks an exchange of angry words, which could then lead to tears, resistance, and ultimatums to our partner. Once a wound is activated in us, it becomes difficult to resolve the issue at hand.

The experience of listening and communicating truthfully often dissolves into accusations of who did what to whom, who's winning the argument, and who has the control. If this happens, we find ourselves on an emotional rollercoaster in which our negative tendencies surface, such as shutting down, running away, or fighting back and creating even more conflict. Nothing gets resolved on this track, and we only end up back at the same problem days or weeks later, repeating the argument again.

However, there is an alternative. Utilize Speaking with Truth and the Listening talents to prepare and guide you toward successful resolution in challenging communication territory. If you are practicing the other talents of communication, you will be prepared to skillfully practice Communication During Conflict.

Here are the Steps for Communicating During Conflict:

- If a heated issue arises, wait and let the "heat" in you calm down. This can take a couple of seconds, a minute, an hour, or more. However, don't wait too long. Make time to communicate within the same day.

- Start the conversation by telling your partner there is something you would like to discuss. Ask when would be a good time for both of you to speak about it. Be prepared to talk about it at the time you ask; many people do not like to be left hanging about an issue. Address it now, or let your lover tell you when would be a more appropriate time later that day or evening.

- Once the time that you have agreed upon arrives, the person that has brought up the issue should begin speaking. Communicate your feelings and what you need from your partner.

- Challenge yourself to communicate lovingly through your conflict.

- Be willing to listen to and take into consideration your partner's point of view.

- Allow both people to be heard respectfully. (You may want to use The Talking Stick Ritual detailed in the following pages.)

- Each person can acknowledge the feelings the issue brings up to themselves silently. If desired, you can then communicate them to your partner. The feelings can include: "I'm not good enough," "I am being unfairly judged," etc. Your acknowledgement can dissolve the intensity of your reactive, negative emotions.

- Don't argue just for argument's sake. That's not to say that you will not argue sometimes, but do it within these healthy parameters.

- Communicate toward an amicable solution that includes finding real clarity, coming back to harmony, and taking responsibility together with an action plan for moving forward.

- Don't bring up past arguments and issues during this particular conflict. Stay focused on what is happening now.

- Be willing to let go of your desire to win the argument, and let go of the issue itself afterwards.

Overcoming the Communication of Demands, Criticism, and Control

When we fall in love, we initially adore who our lover is. But before long, we can start to make demands of, criticize, and want to control our partner and our relationship. Why?

We demand because we don't feel we are getting what we need or want. We criticize because something doesn't feel right to us. We control because we feel that some area of our relationship is chaotic, or because we feel we can't control other parts of our life, so we look for control in our relationship.

We do these things because ultimately we feel unfulfilled, unloved, scared, or vulnerable. But when we perpetually focus on what is wrong with our partner, we become addicted to a cycle of drama that eats away at our relationship. Picking at the little things in our relationship is a keen maneuver to keep us in our ego and far away from intimacy and ecstasy. When focusing on what is wrong with our lover and the relationship becomes the norm, we are headed down the road of destroying our love.

Taoist love artists deal with the underlying issues and alchemize the emotions they carry. This means to transform heavier, negative emotions into positive emotional gold as described earlier in Part One, Transforming Negative Emotions That Block Intimacy as well as in the upcoming Alchemy of Demands, Criticism, and Control.

Dissolve your negative emotions—such as your lack of love, your fear, your neediness, or your emptiness—and claim positive attributes, which include love for yourself, value of yourself, your own wisdom, and your personal capacity to be fulfilled. You alone are responsible for your emotions, responses, and how you choose to focus on your partner and your relationship on a regular basis. Take responsibility for your emotions. Don't make your lover responsible for them; doing so is incredibly draining on your relationship. Once you have alchemized your emotions and changed *how* you focus, your relationship must and will change for the better.

Alchemy of Demands, Criticism, and Control:

- If you are demanding, begin giving more loving communication and affection to your lover.

- If you are critical, focus on your lover's great qualities. Appreciate and compliment your lover instead of criticizing him or her.

- If you are controlling, resolve and let go of what causes you to feel fearful and out of control in relationship to your lover.

Important: if you are being demanded of, criticized by, or controlled by your lover:

- Take a look at *your* part in the issue.
- Take responsibility where needed in the relationship.
- Honor yourself and know when to say no to unreasonable demands.

Overcoming demands, criticism, and control can bring you greater love and joy, making your relationship more fulfilling. Only then can you experience the ecstasy of loving another by seeing, communicating, and fully recognizing the greatness in each other and the relationship that you share.

Note: if you are being verbally or physically abused:

- Recognize that this is *not* and *never will be* love.
- It is important to seek the help of a qualified counselor to address the reasons that are keeping you in an abusive relationship.
- Do not allow abuse from your partner anymore.
- If you feel in danger, remove yourself from the situation as quickly as possible.

The Talking Stick Ritual

This communication ritual is drawn from the Native American tradition. I was introduced to this method over fifteen years ago and feel that it is one of the most beneficial methods for communication that I have discovered. The Native Americans have a long history of understanding something important about communication. To communicate effectively, each person needs to be fully present with each other and often needs a tool, such as a talking stick, to remain aware of who has the floor to speak.

This ritual can be utilized with any of the talents of communication, but it can be especially helpful with the more challenging ones, such as Speaking the Truth, Listening, and Communication During Conflict. This ritual can also add both a sacred and ceremonial dimension to your communication with your loved one.

Steps for Utilizing The Talking Stick Ritual:

- Sit with your full bodies facing each other.
- Use a talking stick made of wood, which is the tradition of the Native Americans. The stick can be short or long, but it should be light enough to easily hold and pass to each other throughout the communication ritual. This can be a stick you find in the backyard or on a hike. You can decorate it if you wish to give it greater significance in your communication ceremonies.
- Whoever is holding the talking stick—and only that person—has the right to speak.
- Each person takes turns holding the talking stick and speaking while the other listens.
- The listener can choose to hold a shell or bowl to receive the other's words.
- This ritual gives each lover an honor system to work with to have healthy, challenging talks. It also supports both people in having greater mindfulness of what is said and builds confidence that each will be heard when they speak.
- If it has been a heavy discussion, you can empty the bowl or shell at the conclusion of your communication by shaking it outside and then washing it together.
- If it has been a loving discussion, you may wish to keep your bowl or shell—which is symbolically filled with these words, thoughts, and feelings—in a special place in your bedroom or in another sacred spot.

Silent Communication

We usually don't think of silence as communication. But our silence communicates many things to our loved one. Our use of silence can be associated with coldness and withdrawal, but it can also be utilized to create loving rewards.

For instance, we can quickly become aware of how to offer our silence as a form of loving communication to our partner when we want to leave our mind behind, when we are tired, or when silent connectivity is more appropriate and desired, such as to calm down after a stressful day or while grieving or ill.

In silence, couples can enjoy a deep intimacy.

There are many forms of silent communication that you can have with your lover. Some beautiful silence can be shared sitting beside each other, holding hands, taking a walk, looking into each other's eyes, silently lying with each other body to body, or in other ways of your own.

Silent Physical Communication

Holding each other quietly, body to body, offers both partners a strong connection emotionally, physically, and spiritually. This is one of my favorite ways to enjoy the talent of silent communication.

Here's how:

- Find a great place to lie down together.
- Lie in each other's arms silently.
- Sync up your energies by tuning into your partner's breathing beside you.
- Make love with each other, either figuratively or literally, sharing a silent moment of quiet intimacy.
- Relax into each other deeply until there is no sense of separation between you and your lover.

Last Word on the Talent of Communication

Communication is vital to the aliveness of our relationships. Connecting with our partner emotionally through communication on a daily basis is nourishing to every aspect of our relationship and our overall well-being.

By letting our lover in on our thoughts and feelings, and taking loving actions toward them, we dissolve our defenses and become more real and human with one another. Experiencing a variety of these communication talents with our intimate partner is a way of expressing that we care about our lover and are excited about the relationship.

Su Nu was now seated on a swing in the warmth of the afternoon sun in her lush, tropical garden. Her next set of couples were scheduled for a semi-private lesson; these were four students who were at the same level of development and who were excited to embark upon their new lesson together. Each couple also sat on swings, but their swings were built for two. These swings were suspended high in the air like circus trapezes. The teacher instructed each couple to secure their lover's safety strap and to swing together.

As the couples began swinging and enjoying themselves, Su Nu said, "Now let's discuss the ingredients that make up a sacred, dynamic relationship."

The couples, entering a state of lightness and laughter, were all ears.

"A rich and dynamic intimate relationship is a balance of enduring core attributes, stimulating interactions and some imagination.

"Essential attributes create the health, harmony, and the foundation of the relationship. The essential attributes that our relationship possesses are what anchor our relationship in love and allow us to move deeper into intimate union.

"A relationship also needs stimulation, activity, and dynamism, which creates polarity and magnetism between lovers. The stimulating interactions we exchange in a relationship are what give our relationships the spice, zest, magic, and romance that we love."

"Would an essential interaction be securing each other and a dynamic interaction be what we are doing now?"

shouted one of the bright young women as she swung to new heights with her lover.

"Exactly," replied the Immortal.

"This is fun," said another couple.

"You are starting to understand how to renew and reinvigorate your intimate relationship," shouted the Immortal. "Let's continue with this lesson and swing higher!"

Talent 4: Creating a Passionate and Dynamic Relationship

A rich and dynamic intimate relationship is a balance of enduring core attributes, stimulating interactions, and intimate innovation. Here you will learn how to renew and reinvigorate your intimate relationship time and time again. There are many ways we can create a passionate and dynamic relationship. Here are the talents we will cover: Create Magic and Romance by Utilizing Yang; Deepen Intimate Union With Yin; Nurture Love Every Time; The Tao of Keeping Your Balance in Relationship; The Seasons of Loving Another; as well as Sacredly and Ultimately Loving Another.

As stated in the beginning of this book, Yin Yang is the ancient Taoist symbol of balance and harmony between the masculine and feminine energies.

Yang, represented by the white color in the symbol, is the active, demonstrative fire force of energy that heats up, humors, charms, and moves through our relationships. The Yang interactions we exchange in a relationship offer our relationships the passionate, magical, and romantic experiences that we crave.

Yin, represented by the black color in the symbol, is the grounding, receptive water essence that nurtures, soothes, loves, and rejuvenates our relationships. The Yin attributes of our relationship anchor our relationship in love and allow us to move deeper into intimate union with each other.

Create Magic and Romance by Utilizing Yang

Magic and romance are usually abundant in the first few months of an intimate relationship. This is called "the honeymoon stage," where Yang passion and dynamism abound. We easily communicate our love for each other and how happy we are to have found each other. We write love notes, bring each other flowers and treats, prepare each other special meals, recite poetry, sing to and with each other, and set the mood for sensational love.

But once we settle into a relationship, these Yang actions often slip by the wayside, and soon the magic is only an occasional occurrence. It is important to keep magic alive in our relationships so we continue to look forward to our connection and the time we share together.

Lacking Magic and Romance

If we don't have enough magic and romance, what happens to our relationship? It becomes dense, flat, and boring.

There are shadows of our personality—hidden, unconscious aspects of ourselves—that arise when our relationship becomes flat. We often get into arguments to create some form of stimulation, even if it is a negative form.

We can also lose interest and find ourselves looking elsewhere for our excitement. When this happens, we may coast emotionally in the relationship. We may check in emotionally every once in a while but then go elsewhere to have fun.

When there is not enough magic and romance—meaning Yang-stimulating activities and interactions between you and your lover—fun is not a big part of your relationship. This is when your relationship has become flat and dull.

Making Magic

The good news is that the magic has not disappeared altogether—it is just one, or a few, emotionally and sexually stimulating activities away. The stimulation and fulfilling activities that you and your partner generate together, like what you enjoy when you first meet, creates magnetic polarity between you and your loved one. Magnetic polarity is what we generally refer to as the incredible sexy magnetism between the Yang-masculine and Yin-feminine that makes us gravitate toward each other like magnets with a ravishing appetite to connect, love, make love, and bond.

Stimulating Yang Activities and Innovation Creates Magic and Romance

To keep the relationship dynamic, exciting, and magnetic, we need to have stimulating activities, interactions, and innovation. Stimulation and creativity improve and renew your relationship vibrancy, creating magnetic polarity and great chemistry for you both to sizzle. The following are some examples.

Stimulating Yang Activities that Create Magic and Romance:

Personal Growth

Growing personally by developing your own interests and talents as well as your capacity for loving well stimulates new interactions and possibilities in your intimate relationship.

Mutual Growth

Growing together as a couple in shared interests like athletics, cooking, building a family, decorating a home, learning a new language, or becoming love artisans can excite your passion for one another.

Setting and Achieving Shared Goals

Having shared goals with your partner, like achieving a project goal, fitness goal, financial goal, or relationship goal can unite your passions.

Personal Time and Space

Doses of healthy distance between you and your lover do make the heart grow fonder. Take time for yourself to recharge your own batteries, and then come back to the relationship excited to see your partner—and ready for romance.

Shared Time and Space

Sharing quality time together by just being with each other, having fun, being playful, and enjoying intimacy will recharge your relationship.

Romance

You need romance to keep your love life stimulating. Experiencing passion and creativity with each other brings a breath of lightness and flair into your relationship.

Great Dialogue

Opening up to your partner through the Talents of Loving Communication as well as discussing interesting topics with each other regularly will ignite your fire and romance.

Sexual Attraction and Intimacy

Having sexual intimacy regularly keeps your sexual chemistry alive.

Shared Responsibilities

Sharing day-to-day responsibilities, such as household chores, parenting, and errands, can build your intimate connection.

Change

Change is great for a relationship. Change your bed cover annually, change the variety of sexual positions you find yourself in regularly, and appreciate your lover in new ways often to put the fire back in your love life.

Deepen Intimate Union with Yin

A deep intimate union is all about the Yin essentials, the qualities that support health and harmony for both people in the relationship and form the foundation of great love. The more essentials you have, the stronger your relationship will be. Essential attributes create a supportive environment for you to grow and for your love to flourish.

The Yin essential attributes that both lovers bring to the relationship will naturally form the preliminary structure of your relationship. While ideally, both partners will come with the attributes necessary for a healthy relationship, often there are core attributes that will have to be developed in one or both partners to create a satisfying and lasting union.

Absence of the Yin Essentials

Essential attributes secure the relationship. If certain core attributes are missing in a relationship, we can feel unloved, resentful, and unsettled.

When the ground is shaking in our relationship, our shadow can appear. Our shadow is the unconscious behavior that we exhibit out of our feelings of fear, sadness, anger, or insecurity. The shadow behavior in a rocky relationship is feeling the need to control and be rigid. We may feel we have to hold on to our hats and find ourselves wanting to control everything that our lover does. This shadow behavior is a negative way of attempting to anchor ourselves and the relationship, and it can drive our partner to the other end of the spectrum with even more unloving and unsettling actions.

Achieving the Union You Want

You can build the kind of relationship that will feed your well-being by developing the essential attributes that make up a great relationship. The objective is to create a harmonious relationship that supports both partners, rather than a dramatic relationship that wreaks havoc. These Yin attributes will give you a solid foundation that will preserve the health and harmony in your relationship.

Essential Yin Attributes That Deepen Intimate Union:

Love
A healthy intimate union begins with love. Love is also what sustains a great relationship over time.

152

Affection
The loving connection that you share through affection
your love, and the foundation of your relationship.

Honesty
A commitment to being honest with your partner through
with one another.

Trust
Without trust, there can be no love. Trust is fundamental to
nership. If your relationship is filled with trust, you will fee
to excel as an individual. You will also discover more inspiration for passion and romance to
flourish in your relationship.

Respect
The act of respect for your lover and your relationship supports both in growing stronger.

Acceptance
Acceptance of each other creates a harmonious dynamic within your relationship. You may
have many goals that you want to achieve in your relationship; moving toward them is invaluable to your relationship. That said, it is also important to accept and appreciate who you are
now and the relationship you currently have.

Willingness
Your availability to be open and present for each other in a relationship defines your current
state of willingness to love. Willingness is the softening of your resistance in order to move
deeper into true love.

Responsibility
Responsibility means doing what you say you will do. It is contributing and actively engaging
in the life experiences you share with your partner. Being a responsible partner in your relationship allows an ease and relaxation to permeate your connection.

ased on an equal share of giving and receiving is a healthy relationship. that are one-sided—where one person dominates by using controlling and behavior—are unhealthy and unequal.

mitment

Commitment is the foundation of a relationship. Your commitment to one another is fundamental to the success you will experience in forming a deep, loving, and fulfilling intimate union.

Nurture Love Every Time

We all have qualities that we can develop to increase our capacity for sharing and creating the love we want to enjoy again and again in our relationships. But these qualities might be different for each partner.

Let's check out where you are strong and where you need to develop in your love relationship. If you are not currently in a relationship, look at your past relationships. By utilizing this model, you can check in to see where you are in your experience as a lover and how you are contributing to the health or disharmony of your current relationship, or how you did contribute in the past.

Ask yourself:

- Are you stronger with initiating Yang interactions and activities and creating magic and romance?

- Or are you stronger in your developed Yin essentials that create a foundation of health and harmony for your relationship?

- Do you need to increase certain skills as a lover? If so, which ones?

- What is working and what isn't in your relationship?

- Where could your relationship get stronger?

Once you have answered these questions and have determined where your strengths and weaknesses are in creating a sacred, passionate relationship, you can utilize the following suggestions to develop the areas where you could even be stronger.

Use the list of Yang activities and Yin essentials on a regular basis to check in on the health of your love life. Apply more Yin or Yang attributes where your relationship is lacking to avoid it becoming boring or unsettled. In this way, you will always be able to create an exciting relationship again and again with your lover!

If you are experiencing a crisis in your relationship, check in even more frequently—weekly or even daily—to build your Yin and Yang attribute muscles to support you in having a healthier and more passionate relationship. If you have been trying to build your attributes and find you need more support, work with a professional counselor.

The Tao of Keeping Your Balance in Relationship

All of us come into a relationship with specific desires and needs. We also come with natural abilities for giving and receiving, as well as a predisposition for responding to relationship stimuli. But, as we have discussed throughout Creating a Passionate, Dynamic Relationship, we can also cultivate our abilities for loving well if they are lacking. These abilities determine how balanced we are in our relationship. Finding our balance and sharing a healthy reciprocation of giving and receiving in a relationship is the next talent of loving another.

Healthy Balance

What is a healthy balance in a relationship?

How we respond when we are exposed to new stimuli—such as hearing surprising news, both good and bad; taking on more responsibility in our lives; having a stressful day; or disagreeing with our lover—will all show where and how we are balanced.

When new stimuli enter our relationship, we can become emotional, sensitive, and reactive. Being centered in our relationship means knowing that our feet are on the ground and we can handle the situation. How quickly we can come back to feeling like ourselves tells us how naturally centered we are. However, we can learn how to avoid getting blown off center by recognizing when we are tilting off balance and then gently bringing ourselves back to center.

From a Taoist perspective, giving and receiving in harmony with our innermost self is the key to having a healthy balance. In other words, whenever we give and receive, we must respond from our center to develop a healthy, balanced dynamic in our relationship with another.

Giving and Receiving from Your Center

If you have ever found yourself feeling drained in a relationship, this means you have left your center in the process of giving and receiving. The Taoists call our center of balance the dantien. This main energy reservoir is located approximately two inches below the navel. If we give from this centered place—or a natural feeling to give—then the act of giving feels healthy and joyful. If we give from outside of our center, which is a place of feeling we *have to* or *should* give, then we will feel drained and resentful.

The same is true of receiving. If we have discomfort receiving, then we are not at center. When we are truly at center our resistance to receiving falls away, leaving us capable of valuing and enjoying the fruits that we receive in love.

I often use a Fit for Love exercise to demonstrate staying centered when you are giving and receiving in love. In this Tai Chi movement, you will be able to see within the body what your natural tendency is for giving and receiving. It is also a wonderful exercise to practice the essence of giving and receiving with your lover.

Tai Chi of Love—Giving and Receiving Exercise

Purpose:

We usually are conditioned in the way we give and receive love. We may give too much love and lose our footing, or we may feel uncomfortable with receiving love and therefore shut down our ability to receive it at all. This Tai Chi exercise is an opportunity to look at our ability to both give and receive love and find a healthy balance to doing both in our lives. You can practice it alone or facing your partner to observe and develop the way you give and receive from each other.

Practice:

- If you are practicing alone, follow all the steps, just leaving out those steps mentioned for a partner. If you are practicing with your partner, face your partner. Stand a couple of feet apart. Each person starts with the right foot facing forward and the other at a forty-five-degree angle behind them. Rock forward, bending the knee toward the front toe.

- Now bend your knee in the back and rock backward. Repeat several times, moving both forward and backward.

- Bend the arms slightly at the elbow, flex your hands, and move forward, bending the knee in front. Feel yourself giving love to your lover as you move forward.

- With your arms still bent slightly at the elbow, bend your wrists so that the fingertips are pointing straight ahead.

- Draw the hands back until they are aligned with the elbows. Take in love from your lover as you move back, bending the back knee.

- Notice where you feel most comfortable. Is it in giving to your lover, or is it in receiving from your lover?

- Remember: don't bend your knee past your toes as you move forward. This is a sign you are out of center. Soften and relax as you move back, keeping your alignment centered. Hold your center as you move forward to give to your lover and also as you move back to receive love.

- Repeat three to nine times to enhance your balance in giving and receiving love.

You can discuss with your lover the experience of how you both are giving and receiving after this exercise or think about it on your own if you have practiced alone.

The following are several dynamics that can be at play in the process of giving and receiving in a relationship. They can be supportive to your discussion.

Healthy Ebb and Flow

When you focus on giving and receiving from your center, you begin to develop a natural ebb and flow of giving and receiving in a relationship that is nurturing and healthy for both partners.

Overcoming Tendencies to Give or Take Too Much

Our tendency to give too much in a relationship is based on our insecurity that we will not be loved if we do not give and give and give—and, on the other hand, that we do not deserve to receive what we are given. Coming into a fuller state of feeling worthy of love will help us overcome the tendency to leave our center and overcompensate in a relationship.

Taking too much comes from our feelings that we aren't getting enough of what we need, and we feel we must grasp for more love, more attention, more affection, or more appreciation from our partner. It is important to take action to nurture ourselves and discuss this dynamic with our lover to create a healthier dynamic of receiving in love.

This would be a good time to journal about your experience, including the feelings, sensations, and realizations that arose during the Tai Chi of Love exercise.

Healthy Losing Yourself

With everything just said about creating a healthy balance in your relationship, it is also a wonderful activity to sometimes lose yourself—meaning your ego self—with someone you love. However, this is a process of being very present and centered as you simultaneously expand your consciousness into the state of ecstasy and bliss with your lover. This can be experienced while making love or by celebrating your relationship together in another meaningful way, such as during one of the talents of communication. These activities offer opportunities for healthy experiences of losing yourself and becoming one with another.

The Seasons of Loving Another

Through our journey of loving another, we go through seasons of change. All lovers face successes and challenges in their personal growth cycles and in their partnership with each other, all of which present opportunities for change.

When a lover is going through an emotional process, such as a specific stage of a career, beginning a family, or experiencing an illness, certain aspects of intimacy can become less prioritized, and others can become more prioritized. For instance, if one partner is experiencing an illness, sex will most likely become less of a priority, and loving care and a positive mental exchange will become more of a priority.

This can feel very challenging to each lover. It can cause either lover to question the feeling of stability in the relationship. It is important to communicate clearly when new relationship experiences arise, in order to move through the processes they offer us with love for each other, harmony, and balance.

Sacred Lovers can hold the space for the other to move through the seasons of love so the relationship can grow in new ways. When new situations arise, it is vital to look at different ways that we can show love to each other to nurture the present moment in our relationship. Perhaps that may mean that a new talent of loving another is being called forth to be expressed more fully in your love and intimacy. It can also mean that you will spend more time nurturing a specific area of your relationship. This is often necessary when a greater focus is being called forth—for instance, to heal and recover from giving birth, having an illness, or working through a demanding career situation.

It is important to honor our cycles in a relationship.

However, if a cycle has lasted for an extended period of time, and it does not seem as if you and your partner can find your way out of it, this could undermine your relationship. It is then wise to seek the help of a counselor, who can help support you through this challenging personal or relationship process.

Your and your partner's ability to flow smoothly through the seasons of your relationship with support and love for each other will keep the love that you share alive and rich. Over time, the loving experiences you share during cycles of change—in such areas as your sexuality, loving connectivity, communication, and spiritual union—will carry even greater passion, meaning, and satisfaction for you both.

The Lack of Love

We may carry the impression that love is painful, heartbreaking, dramatic, and emotionally exhausting. But these are not experiences of love. They are, in fact, *the experiences of a lack of love*.

It is the absence of love that causes pain.

When we are not capable of or skilled at loving, we create heartache, or we abuse and control. When we don't fully feel love for ourselves, we long for fulfilling love. We also excuse our lover's unloving behaviors and accept a lack of relationship fulfillment and hardship as part of the love experience. But instead of compromising ourselves and not getting what we want in love, we can choose to have the experience of Sacred Love in our lives by stating what we need, not compromising on the important elements that are key to our fundamental happiness, getting help from a counselor if needed, and knowing if and when it is time to say good-bye.

Some Intimate Relationships Are Not Meant to Last

If the difficulties outweigh the rewards in the relationship you have, it most likely means that it is not the right relationship for both of you. This doesn't mean that your partner wasn't a Sacred Lover.

Every relationship is not meant to last a lifetime. Some are meant to take us through periods of learning and cycles of our life, then end, or perhaps transform into something else: a friendship, a lesson learned, or the end of a stage of life in which you can not grow any further. Some relationships are meant to be shared the distance of a lifetime. It is important to be able to recognize the difference. If you are faced with needing to end a relationship, utilize your abilities through the talent of loving another to end it consciously with love, respect, and integrity. This way you will honor the journey of love that you have shared with your partner.

Sacredly and Ultimately Loving Another

We have learned that a great intimate relationship is filled with love. It invites, excites, and fills us up with love physically, emotionally, mentally, and spiritually. This kind of love shines the brightest light where there is still an absence of love inside of us and massages us and caresses us into experiencing the abundant ecstasy of even more love. Having a great relationship makes all of life much easier, as it offers us more energy to utilize and direct in all our life purposes.

The only things that keep us from having great and Sacred Love in our lives is our lack of love for ourselves, our resistance to intimacy, and the skills we need to develop in order to experience it.

Sacredly loving another is a daily experience of appreciation and loving action. It is a nurturing reciprocation of giving and receiving, as well as working together to resolve challenges. It is also shared joy, happiness, and intimate relationship fulfillment. To achieve this ultimate experience of love, you have to love yourself in totality and be able to love your lover with this same, all-encompassing wholeness.

When we let down our intimate armor, reveal the full brightness of our self-love, and mindfully apply the talent of loving another to our relationships, we will meet great love in our partnerships and feel time and time again the empowering and transformative experience of true and Sacred Love.

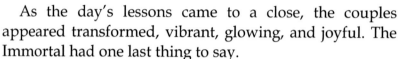

As the day's lessons came to a close, the couples appeared transformed, vibrant, glowing, and joyful. The Immortal had one last thing to say.

"Each Talent of Loving Another has the power to positively transform your connection to the love, pleasure, and intimate union you share with your loved one. I encourage you to utilize these talents to deepen and more fully enjoy your intimate relationship."

Then the Immortal vanished, not to be seen until the next day. At the place where she had stood, a luminous glow prevailed. It would remain there until the next morning as a guiding light for her students, so they could enjoy the garden throughout the night.

THE ART OF
SACRED LOVE-MAKING
PART THREE

In this final section, The Art of Sacred Love-Making, you will be taken through an erotic journey of a Sacred Love-Making experience. Powerful ingredients will be given to accentuate and intensify your pleasure and love, and secret methods for bringing the sacred into lovemaking are revealed. This art of intimate wisdom adds even more naturalness, wildness, meaning, and sexual satisfaction to the enjoyment of your most intimate relationship.

From Sex to Sacred Love-Making

While sex of itself can be very physically enjoyable and pleasing to the senses, sex can be much more than that.

Sacred Love-Making is the art of bringing your body, heart, mind, and spirit into the act of lovemaking. The more you can bring of yourself to the lovemaking experience, the finer the quality and abundance of the pleasure, satisfaction, and ecstasy you can enjoy. The more present you can be, the more alive you, your lover, and the sexual experience you share will become.

You may ask why sex as described above is disturbingly rare or totally absent and the understanding of sex's sacred dimensions all but lost for centuries. You may find the answer surprising, because it can be found in the midst of one of the world's most well-known stories, the Garden of Eden.

I would like to walk you through this story from the perspective of how it relates to the foundation of some of our most formative beliefs and often present behaviors of sexuality.

What Happened in the Garden of Eden?

In the legendary story of the Garden of Eden, Adam and Eve were created "naked and not ashamed" to love each other and enjoy existence in an earthly paradise. The story goes that one day, the beautiful, erotic Eve encounters a serpent. The serpent advises her to eat from the Tree of Knowledge, which God had told her and Adam not to eat from. The serpent tells her, "For God knows that in the day you eat of it your eyes will be opened and you will be like God."—Genesis, 3:5. When Eve realizes that this tree could offer her God's wisdom, she eats the fruit and offers it to her husband to eat. Then, "the eyes of them both were opened."—Genesis 3:7

What were Adam and Eve's eyes opened to?

God seemed to be frightened of what they could see; he said, "Behold, the man is become as one of us, to know good and evil: and now, lest [if] he put forth his hand, and take also of the tree of life, and eat, and live forever."—Genesis 3:21. In other words, eating this fruit of wisdom caused Eve and Adam to see and become like God to obtain powerful gifts previously attributed only to God. (This often rare, but possible human state is referred to as spiritual awakening or enlightenment.)

For taking the advice of the serpent and eating of the Tree of Knowledge, Eve and Adam are banished from their earthly garden, and God curses them. Among the curses: for man and woman to have hostility between them, for the woman to feel suffering in childbearing, and for the husband to rule over the wife.—Genesis 3:15-16

This legendary story that has spun three of the world's largest religions, Judaism, Islam, and Christianity, offers great symbolism of the shift from the once widespread reverence, beliefs, and methods of the Sacred Feminine to those of the Sacred Masculine.

The Sacred Feminine

In modern times, we know very little about the Sacred Feminine, but for thousands of years, before Genesis was ever written, civilizations from around the world honored her. According to Riane Eisler's well-known book *Chalice and the Blade*, from ancient Greece and Egypt to Mesopotamia, Ireland, China, and India, the Sacred Feminine—also called "Goddess"—was revered for her life-giving properties. She was associated with the beauty and abundance of nature, the physical human body, sexuality, creativity, and ecstatic joy. These cultures revered the spirit inherent in all of nature. They connected to the Sacred Feminine through the cycle of seasons, trees and fruits of the garden, by befriending the animals, and honoring women. These cultures also carried the mysteries of the inner world. And the serpent, who symbolized an important inner mystery, was a close friend of the Goddess. She honored and utilized the serpent's sacred wisdom of awakening transformation and ecstasy.

As stated briefly in Part One: The Sacred Lover, the serpent throughout many early world traditions has symbolized the awakening of the sexual energy. Once the serpent was awakened, it could travel up the spine, known as "The Tree of Life" (the tree from which Eve and Adam had not yet eaten), and illuminate the spirit in a state of ecstasy. The setting of the Garden of Eden was directly symbolic of the life-giving forces and the erotic rites held sacred by these feminine-revering cultures.

The Sacred Masculine

The Sacred Masculine has been revered for approximately the last seven thousand years. According to *Chalice and the Blade* author Riane Eisler, the "Father God" originally appeared during the invasions of Indo-European warrior-priests (including the well-known Semites), who took over the lands of Canaan, and other warrior-priests who spread into Europe and Asia Minor.

The Sacred Masculine is represented by heaven and sun, or Father, as well as the Son and Holy Ghost. The teachings of the Sacred Masculine focused on the consequences of one's outer deeds and actions. It offered an experience of life beyond earth with the reward of a heavenly paradise after death. To connect with God, one would need to connect with the Father in heaven—or, in many cases, a male representative of his teachings.

The Results

These different sets of beliefs brought the traditions of the Sacred Feminine and Masculine at odds with each other. In their showdown in the story of the Garden of Eden, the Sacred Masculine ideology wins out. The mystical ways of the Sacred Feminine—including a reverence for earthly life; the belief that nature, sexuality, and spirituality were all integral; and the transcendent powers of the serpent—were replaced. In came the Sacred Masculine paradigm that elevated the beliefs that the earthly and spiritual worlds were separate, that one's physical life would determine whether one would eventually enter the heavenly paradise, and that the serpent was ultimately evil. The story of the Garden of Eden was the most important literary entrée of the Sacred Masculine into the global collective consciousness.

This historical account is not written to judge the Sacred Feminine tradition over the Sacred Masculine tradition or masculine over feminine. There is a place and need for both. This account is only provided to understand a broader perspective of many people's intimate history and what elements may have played a fundamental role in shaping who we are. For it is only possible to move forward once we understand the origins of our intimate thought processes.

The Sexual Aftermath

Unfortunately, this transition in belief systems began to wreak havoc on sexual relations and intimate relationships in general. People began to believe that having sex, and the human body itself, was something to be ashamed of. Sex became about external objectification rather than an internal, uplifting, and ecstatic spiritual rapture to reach divine union. Sexual women were disapproved of and regarded as whores. The belief that women and their sexuality needed to be dominated ushered in a harmful era of male dominance over women. Intimate relationships, families, communities, and the world at large have suffered for it. Ultimately, sex wasn't sacred anymore.

Sacred Coupling

In order to write Part Three: The Art of Sacred Love-Making it was important to address the spiritual side of our relationship to sex, including how this religious history has played its part in shaping and hindering our sexual and intimate expression, which leads to the underlying significance of this section. Fortunately today, there is an undercurrent of movement within different faiths to approach sex with a healthier attitude.

In Part Three, we will explore how to bring the sacred back into the sexual experience. We will take this sacred journey by embracing the essences of both the inner-mystery feminine orientation to love and sex along with the external-sensory masculine orientation. By honoring *both* the feminine and the masculine ways, lovers can meet one another anew—awakening sexual pleasure at the physical level, experiencing more love and joy at the emotional level, and reaching ecstatic rapture at the spiritual level. We can then begin to experience the sacred occurring within our lovemaking, for sacred coupling can guide us toward greater internal well-being, allowing us to create a more harmonious and satisfying sexual intimate relationship overall.

Let's begin …

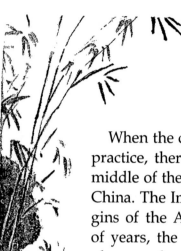

When the couple arrived for their Sacred Love-Making practice, there was a visual projection suspended in the middle of the garden displaying images of erotic art from China. The Immortal's voice was heard narrating the origins of the Art of Sacred Love-Making. "For thousands of years, the Tao has helped couples experience greater pleasure, love, ecstasy, and spiritual fulfillment during lovemaking …"

The couple watched and listened intently.

The Immortal appeared in the garden at the end of the screening. She addressed the couple with a bow, and they bowed back to her. She then motioned for them to sit with her by the cascading waterfall that flowed into a private lagoon in the garden.

"Your artistic ability creates Sacred Love-Making," said the Immortal. "You have already developed many talents in your training as a Sacred Lover, and you will be putting them to use throughout your journey of Sacred Love-Making.

"The gifts you demonstrate with your heart, body, mind, and spirit can invite in the sacred experience and enrich your enjoyment of lovemaking. The talents of your body are exhibited through physical expressions. The talents of your heart fill these physical expressions with passion, playfulness, tenderness, and strength. The talents of your mind are demonstrated in your willingness to grow and your knowledge of the art. Your spirit's talent is in its awareness and in the expansive new possibilities it offers to another in the moment of lovemaking. What artistic talents do you want to attain for Sacred Love-Making?" asked the teacher.

The female student answered first. "I want to connect more fully. I want to experience sexual, emotional, and spiritual union during lovemaking."

The male student then said, "I want to stay present during the pleasure and ecstasy of lovemaking. I would also like to learn the art of lovemaking rituals."

"Well, then you are ready for the waterfall," said the Immortal.

The waterfall immediately started to flow inside of each of the lovers. Both jumped up, thinking they would get wet. But the water was not wetting them at all. It continued to flow through them, even though they had moved.

"Sit, my dears," encouraged the teacher. "The water is not physical water but ephemeral water that renews and restores. It is utilized to clear your thoughts and melt away any fear or tension present in your body. Relax and surrender to the flow."

The couple sat again, relaxed, and followed the instructions. The Immortal continued.

"You are about to enter into a new realm of intimate exploration. It is a doorway that can lead you to greater intimate joy than you have ever known."

The rock wall behind the waterfall then opened into an exquisite hidden sanctuary that the couple had never seen in all their months in the garden. As the Immortal left the couple to enter it alone, she said, "You will find all that you need for your next lessons inside. Enjoy your journey."

Sacred Love-Making Artistry

Sacred Love-Making is the ultimate opportunity to wield your skills as a sexual artist and alchemist and to take pleasure in a majestic journey of the erotic terrain you share with your lover. Your ability to be fully present, create beautiful love rituals, and infuse more passion into your love play will add a more meaningful atmosphere to your lovemaking. Then, as you cultivate the sexual elixir and learn to circulate and exchange your sexual energy together, you can produce the sexual alchemical experiences that will make your lovemaking a truly sacred art.

This art is a celebration of love for you and your lover. Each art presented is a Sacred Love-Making experience unto itself. Release the need to reach any particular goal during a lovemaking experience, and enjoy the adventure of sacredly and sexually loving one another.

Art 1: Creating a Harmonious and Sacred Space

Using the principles of Feng Shui, here you will learn the rituals of how to balance the chi in your intimate environment to enhance and foster love. Your environment reflects your psychological state in all ways. You can learn to increase the positive flow of love energy to heighten your intimate experience by: Creating a Sacred Space and Sacred Intentions, as well as Harmonizing Heart, Body, and Soul.

Creating a Sacred Space

A beautiful, sensuous environment makes us feel instantly welcome, tranquil, and in touch with our senses. Love artists create beautiful, compelling, sacred spaces for love and lovemaking by utilizing the art of Feng Shui.

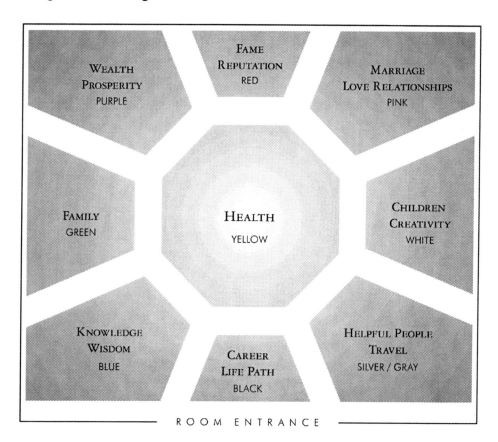

What is Feng Shui?

Feng Shui is the Taoist art of arranging our personal environment into harmonious patterns. This art is designed to attain serenity with nature, bringing greater balance and happiness into our life.

172

Feng Shui Can Be Utilized for Love

Feng Shui can balance the chi, meaning energy, in your surroundings to enhance love. Our personal environment expresses our emotional, physical, and psychological state towards love. You can create a more loving, nurturing environment in your home by understanding the flow of energy for love in your personal space.

The area of your home in the far right corner away from your main front door is designated as holding the energy space for love. Notice if this is an area that you naturally move toward to enjoy lovemaking experiences. Always keep this area well tended and uncluttered.

In the Feng Shui chart, you will see that the color pink is noted for the relationship area of your home. This is because pink is recognized to boost the energy of love and romance. You can utilize variations of this color, such as scarlet, royal purple, sunset orange, or deep rose, to achieve your personal preference and bring warmth and passion to this area. You can even add fresh flowers in a desirable pink tone.

Perhaps place a romantic scenic photo in your space, or one of you and your lover, to enhance the harmonious and abundant love filling your home and life.

If this area of your home is not suited for lovemaking, still keep the area well tended with elements that communicate love and romance. This will enhance and support the love vibration in your home. Then move toward the area of your home you are most likely to make love in and begin creating your sacred space for lovemaking.

Utilize the Feng Shui chart to help you design a sensual and loving home and ideal room for lovemaking.

Creating a sacred space prepares an atmosphere for you and your lover that is conducive for pleasure and love. Doing so allows each person to sink into the intimate space more fully. As a result, the unfolding of your lovemaking experiences will take place harmoniously, passionately, and beautifully.

Your Sacred Space

This easy and beautiful ritual of Sacred Love-Making will set the tone for a meaningful and artistic celebration of your love.

First, choose a room that is right for you for your Sacred Love-Making experiences, such as your living room or bedroom, and transform it into your permanent love sanctuary. (View the following suggestions for ideas and inspiration). Bring into play whatever inspires you.

For a specific Sacred Love-Making occasion, enhance your love sanctuary with the help of your loved one by taking a few minutes to refresh your sacred space and adorn it with some newly inspired sensual love elements.

Here Are Activities and Items to Help Beautify Your Sacred Space:

- Clean and freshen the room that you have chosen. Open a window or door to let fresh air inside.
- Remove any items left over from past relationships from your bedroom or love sanctuary.
- Create an environment that will be comfortable and enjoyable for two. Make sure there are two sides of the bed that are easily accessible. Have two candles, two glasses, two pillows, and so forth.
- Beautify your room in preparation for Sacred Love-Making with elements that inspire love and sensuality.
- Light candles.
- Burn aromatherapy oils or incense.
- Use rich, deep colors as a foundation, such as gold, peach, chocolate, and silver, to create a sexy atmosphere.
- Use passionate (relationship energizing) colors as accents, such as contrasting strong reds, purples, oranges, and pinks to create a romantic atmosphere.
- Place your favorite flowers—such as one of my favorites, Casablanca lilies—in your room or scatter rose petals on the bed and floor.
- Play sexy or romance inspiring music (Please see the appendix at the back of the book for a list of music my clients and I have especially enjoyed!)
- Place some silk or velvet pillows on the bed, floor, or both.
- Transform your room into a sacred harmonious and sensual space for lovemaking.
- Adorn yourself with a beautiful robe or bedroom attire that makes you feel sensual.
- Make sure your attire is comfortable to move around in for the beginning of your Sacred Love-Making journey.
- Begin by sitting across from your lover.
- Relax into your love sanctuary.

Sacred Intentions

The ritual of intention is like that performed in a sensuous Chinese tea ceremony.

In a Chinese tea ceremony, the participants set a mindful intention for the enjoyment of the tea. In successive rounds, the server passes around tiny cups of exotic teas for attendants to smell, taste, and experience. The attendants then savor each tea. Without even realizing it in just minutes the graceful ceremony produces an effect of ease, relaxation, and deep pleasure for the attendants.

Attention fully fixed on one's purpose can create a magical romantic experience. An intention for Sacred Love-Making can set in motion a dynamic dialogue between you and your partner. The purpose for creating a Sacred Love-Making intention is to enhance love and sexual intimacy in your relationship.

Some people shy away from asking for what they want in intimacy, for fear of being criticized or dismissed. Others have found it difficult to envision an experience different than what they have historically had during lovemaking. If any one of these have been true for you, challenge yourself to ask for what you want with an intention. Making a sacred intention can greatly support you in asking for and experiencing more of what you want in lovemaking.

Sacred Intention Ritual

Guidelines:

Creating an intention with your partner before lovemaking attunes both lovers and sets the atmosphere for what you both desire. See your lover in their most exalted state, as an Emperor or Empress. Recognize that you *both* hold the space for this sacred experience of lovemaking to take place.

Practice:

While looking lovingly into each other's eyes, bring your hands to your own hearts in a prayer position in preparation for making an intention together for lovemaking. You may want to formulate one intention together verbally, or make two intentions individually, perhaps silently. The experience can be different each time.

For Example:

- Intend to enjoy greater pleasure with one another.
- Intend to open more fully in your emotional connection to your lover.

- Intend to receive physical, emotional, and spiritual satisfaction from this Sacred Love experience.

- You may want to create a statement together that you can always make before each Sacred Love-Making experience, such as
  I honor my heart, body, mind, and spirit. My lover, I honor your heart, body, mind, and spirit. I respect the sacredness of this lovemaking experience that we are now co-creating. May it satisfy our bodies, open our hearts, awaken our minds and spirits, and bond us even more deeply to each other in love and pleasure.

- After you have made your intention(s), let go and stay open to all possibilities.

- Bow respectfully with love to each other.

- You may then want to toast each other with a sip of wine or juice.

- Begin Sacred Love-Making.

Harmonizing Heart, Body, and Soul

We have just explored two powerful rituals to help you create a space of beauty and harmony and to invite greater clarity and sacredness into your lovemaking. This next lovemaking ritual will bring you and your lover face to face to meet each other in a new light. This new space is the inner realm of heart, body, and soul. You are about to create a framework of relating to each other that will be incredibly powerful to both of you. It is erotic, intimate, and non-verbal.

Harmonizing heart, body, and soul with your lover brings you into an enhanced emotional and high-vibrational space to savor pleasure and intimacy with each other. This space is inclusive and beyond the limits of your conscious mind. In this ritual, each partner can gently open their heart, body, and spirit to each other to experience a deeper connection during this beautiful moment. This is a wonderful way to begin Sacred Love-Making.

In the Taoist tradition, feeling aroused in the heart is attributed to the feminine, or Yin, energy, for it is said that a woman becomes sexually stimulated by first feeling a heart connection with her lover. The Taoists explain that the male energy initially becomes stimulated through feeling a sexual connection with his lover, and then that sexual connection can lead the male energy to open his heart. All individuals have both masculine and feminine energies inside that play out in different ways to different degrees.

In this ritual, you will honor both the male and female sexual energy responses by establishing a connection and pathway between each lover's heart and sexual centers.

As discussed in Part One, our hearts, bodies, and spirits also carry certain vibrations, depending on our physical, emotional, and psychological states. In this ritual, we want to consciously harmonize our vibrations with our lover's vibrations to awaken greater magnetic attraction to each other in the moment.

At times, it may feel difficult to open your heart, or consciously connect sexually with your lover, as you may have experienced hurt, rejection, or pain in these areas with your current lover or in a past relationship. In these cases, personal practice with the skills mentioned throughout this book—such as Confronting the Ghosts of Intimacy in Part One and Claiming the Courage to Love in Part Two—can greatly enhance your ability to open up to your lover now.

Ritual of Harmonizing Heart, Body, and Soul:

To Begin:
- Face each other and sit up straight. Let your breathing be natural.
- Look into each other's eyes and smile.

- Take your time and relax into the connection you share with your partner.
- Recognize what you love about your lover and what makes your partner special to you.

Soul to Soul:
- Appreciate the divine essence of your partner.
- Appreciate your spiritual connection together.
- See and feel yourself connecting to your partner's spirit by looking into each other's eyes for one minute or more.

Heart to Heart:
- Each person places his or her left hand on the other partner's heart.
- Smile and feel your partner's heart.
- Allow your touch to help soften and open your partner's heart.
- Feel both your hearts opening, connecting, and harmonizing to receive love.
- Allow heart energy to flow back and forth between each other by breathing into your own heart and then exhaling into your lover's heart for at least a minute.
- Smile.

Body to Body:
- Each of you brings your right hand to your partner's sexual center without attempting to stimulate each other.
- Smile. Feel yourself connecting with your partner sexually.
- Be aware of how your sexual connection feels.
- Be aware of the sexual chemistry you share.
- Feel the sexual energy flowing back and forth between each of you as you breathe into your own sexual center and then exhale into your lover's sexual center. Continue to breathe in this pattern with your lover for a minute or more.
- Smile, and enjoy the feeling of pleasure.

Two Become One:

- Continue to breathe.

- Make sure that the love you give to yourself on the inhale matches the love you give to your lover on the exhale. Note: we can often give our lover much more than we give ourselves or, conversely, give ourselves more than we are giving our lover. This ritual can help create an *equal* balance for both your lover and you.

- Look into each other's eyes and connect spiritually.

- Feel yourself becoming relaxed and your connection growing stronger.

- Send a loving smile to your partner.

- In this moment, intend for any resistance you have toward love and pleasure to dissolve.

- Allow your heart to melt into pure love.

- Feel your sexual response begin to lift, percolate, and heat up.

- Feel the two of you harmonizing, vibrating, and magnetizing each other—heart, body, and soul.

- Stay in this state with each other for two to ten minutes.

- Then you may choose to either continue with more foreplay or begin making love.

With this ritual, it becomes easier to surrender to the moment and show vulnerability to your partner. Beginning lovemaking in a connected state increases both your and your lover's emotional and physical capacities for pleasure.

The Immortal, perceiving that the couple was ready for the next art, allowed her voice to travel through the sanctuary, telling them a bedtime story.

"The crimson faced Emperor shyly said, 'Please enlighten me on the Tao of sexual response.' My immortal sister replied this time, saying, 'When Yin and Yang act harmoniously, the male will be firm and powerful, and the female will open to him. Yin brings joy. Yang brings excitement and desire.'

"When these two are in accord, a passionate, effortless, fluid coupling takes place.

"If Yin and Yang are out of balance, with either too much or too little of either polarity, then sexual response is forced and will not ignite correctly or last long."

"How does one know what polarity is out of balance?" asked the male partner.

"Good question," replied the Immortal with a touch of playfulness in her voice.

"First, take a look at your relationship dynamic," she instructed. "Is the relationship governed by excessive activity … rest and relaxation … or a balance of both action and relaxation?

"Then take into account both of you as individuals. Does one of you have more Yang—active, driving energy—and one more Yin—receptive, relaxed energy? While each polarity is associated with either male or female, they are not necessarily gender specific."

The couple looked at each other, feeling the teacher was reading their minds.

"In love and intimacy, a man can exhibit more Yin energy, and a woman can exhibit more Yang. In this case, or in the opposite case, the chemistry would be a match. If both exhibit excessive Yang in love, then the chemistry will combust. If both lovers have excessive Yin energy, the chemistry will be soft and relaxed and then tend to dissipate. A healthy sexual response is awakened when the Yin and Yang energies of the couple are in balance for intimacy."

The couple looked a little concerned.

The Immortal continued. "By respecting and nurturing the polarities, just like the Emperor who discovered how to enjoy a healthy sexual response at each lovemaking encounter, so will you. The following art will help you increase your vibrant sexual response."

The Immortal gave the couple their next instruction to cultivate their intimate use of Yin and Yang in the private bedroom sanctuary.

Art 2: Sparking Magnetic Chemistry

When Yin and Yang act in union and harmony, the result is arousing excitement and joy. Here you will learn how to balance the male/female sexual equation for effortless and passionate sexual chemistry and lovemaking with the following components: Factors for Sparking Magnetic Chemistry, Yin and Yang of Sexual Passion, Emotional Magnetism, Sexual Response and Long-Lasting Lovemaking, as well as Overcoming Being Tired.

Factors for Sparking Magnetic Chemistry

There are several indispensable factors that help us achieve magnetic chemistry for the stimulating arousal, satisfaction, and longevity of lovemaking. Each of these factors is based on the intimate and sexual harmony of Yin and Yang with our lover. These factors include sexual passion, emotional magnetism, and sexual health and endurance.

Sexual Passion

Sexual Passion is the factor that represents the sexual chemistry that we share with our lover. Our ability to understand and utilize the polar principles of Yin (feminine) and Yang (masculine) in our sexual interactions can intensify our sexual heat for one another.

Emotional Magnetism

Emotional Magnetism is the factor that signifies the emotions that we have about sexual expression, as well as the ones we have about our current relationship with our lover. When these relationships are in the right harmony, the result is a magnetizing sexual tango for two.

Sexual Health and Endurance

Sexual Health and Endurance is the health and vitality of our physical bodies that informs our ability to become aroused sexually and determines our continual sexual response throughout lovemaking. Maintaining a healthy body, as well as strengthening the sexual muscles located along the bottom floor of the pelvic diaphragm (see the Sexual Toning exercise detailed in the following pages), adds the stamina needed to enjoy long-lasting sexual satisfaction.

Sparking Magnetic Chemistry is dedicated to developing these factors to ignite the right balance of passion and excitement between you and your lover in every lovemaking encounter.

Yin and Yang of Sexual Passion

Utilize the following list of Yang attributes and corresponding expressions as well as Yin attributes and corresponding experiences to help you create the sexual passion that you desire anytime.

Yang	Expression
Masculine	Express your masculine nature.
Activity	Take action sexually.
Fire	Know when and how to light a fire.
Boiling	Can you bring your lover to a boil?
Mind	Engage your lover with your mind.
Thought	Imagine all the possibilities for sexual artistry.
Individuality	Be an authentic person.
Linear	Have great follow-through.
Pursue	Go to your lover.
Give	Offer your lover gifts of the heart.
Penetrate	Enter the flower.
Excite	Enliven your lover's sexual appetite.
External	Externalize your feelings to your lover.
Shallow	Don't forget the surface of your lover's body.
Light	Lighten your lover's heart with laughter.

Yin	Experience
Feminine	Express your feminine nature.
Relaxation	Relax into the moment of lovemaking.
Water	Bathe in the waters before making love.
Cooling	Do you know when to cool your lover down?
Body	Seduce your lover with your body.
Sensuality	Sensually dance with your lover.
Unity	Surrender to ecstatic love.
Fluid	Go with the flow of an intimate encounter.
Magnetize.	Invite the attention of your lover.
Receive	Receive the abundance of love from your lover.
Open	Open to the stem.

Rest	Restore mind and body.
Internal	Internalize your pleasure upwards.
Deep	Kiss your lover totally.
Dark	Turn down the lights and set the mood.

A Chemical Reaction

A couple must have sexual chemistry to have sexual fulfillment.

Generally, a couple knows they have great natural sexual chemistry before they ever kiss. They may feel sexually aroused in the other's presence. They may think of each other sexually when they are not with each other. But other times, it may take getting to know one another before a couple can recognize the sexual chemistry that they can enjoy together.

Sexual chemistry is what makes our sexual relationships hot, sexy, and really satisfying. If natural sexual chemistry is not present, it can be very difficult to achieve sexual arousal and enjoy a sexual interaction. This can become frustrating and emotionally painful for both partners.

It is important to address this issue if you are having difficulty in this area of your relationship. You may need the help of a qualified counselor or physician to understand the nature of the issue and find your way to creating sexual fulfillment with one another. You may also need to accept that you will not share that area of a relationship with this person. Some intimate relationships can work out without a sexual relationship. But if that isn't true for you, then you will need to move on.

Even with an abundance of natural sexual chemistry, there generally comes a time in every intimate relationship when the chemistry doesn't ignite as immediately as it did in the beginning of the relationship. This does not mean that the spark is gone, but it does mean that it will take a bit more skill to light your sexual fires again. However, with a little know-how, this endeavor can be exceptionally exciting and fun!

In the sexiest relationships, two lovers can engage Yin and Yang's captivating powers for tantalizing results. This means that each lover can switch Yin and Yang roles when they desire. This can be done in big and small ways. For instance, a big choice might include, the man dancing for the woman or the woman pursuing and initiating a sexual encounter. A small but powerfully sexy choice may be for the lovers to switch the side of the bed they sleep on every other night to keep things fresh and exciting.

Lasting sexual attraction is about changing things around and not getting stuck in a routine with your techniques as a lover, or in the dynamics of sex itself. Throw a bit of "crazy" into your repertoire of love play and sexual positions. Have sex outside of your bedroom—in the living room, outdoors, or maybe even at a nice hotel. Bring more of yourself to the sexual experience in new, innovative ways.

Exploring the Yin and Yang powers in your sexual relationship and discovering what and where you need to add more of one element or remove some of the other will help you create the perfect alchemy for a sizzling attraction and a captivating sexual experience. Apply Yin when there is a need for sensuality, flow, and openness. Apply Yang when you need more heat, passion, and pursuit. With practice, you can create great sexual response between you and your lover in each lovemaking encounter.

Emotional Magnetism

Emotional Magnetism is made up of the compelling emotional states tha
the other. We are sexually drawn to our lover's charisma, charm, thoughtfι
tiousness, love, affection, kindness, attentiveness, and positive support. V
from our lover's anger, control, judgment, insensitivity, depression, nega
coldness. How our lover makes us feel about ourselves will either magnetize us toward our
lover for sexual intimacy or distance us from engaging sexually.

Personal Emotions

The emotions that we have around sexual expression are the foundation of emotional magnetism. If we have a majority of positive emotions about enjoying sex, then we will naturally
gravitate toward having a nurturing, fulfilling sexual experience. On the other hand, if we feel
emotionally conflicted about expressing ourselves sexually, it can be a totally different story.
For instance, if we grew up with the belief that sex will lead to heartache, then when we have
sex—whether we are married to our partner or not—we often have not come to terms with sex
as a loving, beautiful, and good experience. In this case, we can have a difficult time becoming
aroused and allowing ourselves to express our sexuality in a healthy, satisfying way.

Relationship Emotions

The state of our day-to-day emotional relationship with our lover also determines the health of
our sexual response. If we are experiencing a joyful and harmonious connection to each other,
we magnetize each other even closer. But if we are feeling criticized or neglected by our lover
during the day or throughout the week, and we do not resolve the issue, then we don't feel like
moving any sexually closer to each other.

Argument Magnetism

We've all watched a scene like this unfold in movies, and some of us may have even experienced it ourselves: two lovers begin to argue, and in the midst of their charged emotions,
wild, sexual passion erupts. This steamy sexual interlude is the effect of opposites—in this
case, strong opposite views—attracting each other and igniting Yin/Yang magnetic polarity
between them. While initially this dynamic can seem really hot, a pattern of fighting to ignite
your sexual chemistry can be emotionally harmful to your relationship. Many times after this
kind of sexual encounter, negative emotions are still present, while the underlying reason for

argument isn't resolved, and your negative feelings can end up cycling back a short time later. Resolving your arguments before engaging sexually will bring you back into a positive emotional magnetic state, which is the ideal state for a healthy sexual encounter.

Truthfulness Can Be Your Best Aphrodisiac

Unresolved emotions create sexual distance. Getting to underlying emotions that have been left unresolved for a period of time can liberate your sexual chemistry with your lover. Being honest about the thoughts and feelings that have taken you away from wanting to connect sexually with your lover can bring you closer together again. Honesty can clear the emotional space between you, so that you can open your heart more and share greater sexual pleasure and ecstasy.

The Demagnetizing Effect of Sexual Secrets

Although sexual truth is amazingly arousing, it can be scary. (See Speaking the Truth in Part Two.) In many intimate relationships, we may start out being honest with our partner, but over time—due to our emotional investment in our relationship—we may become more apprehensive about telling our sexual truths. Our fears can range from fear of getting the cold shoulder, to starting an argument, or worst of all, being abandoned.

If fear wins out a secretiveness or loud silence starts to take root. This can have a deadening effect on an intimate relationship. Being secretive and holding back feelings or actions may seem titillating and safe at first, but inevitably it cuts us off from fully experiencing personal wholeness and enjoying truly fulfilling intimacy in our relationship.

Secretiveness leads to discomfort and pain for the person who is being secretive. When we are secretive, we cannot open up fully, because a lot of our energy is tied up in harboring our secret. Secretiveness also harms the person with whom we are not being honest, as the person is subconsciously aware that he or she also cannot fully open up with us.

Truth makes us feel good about ourselves and helps us feel relaxed and happy. While truthfulness takes courage—at times *great* courage—its payoff is a greater level of sexual desire, excitement, and romantic feelings between partners.

Nurturing your personal and relationship harmony develops a sense of wholeness and well-being in your intimate life that invigorates your sexual response. Pay attention to your emotions as you move through a Sacred Love-Making experience. If any negative emotions present themselves, address them. Recognize that clarity and resolution of your emotions can lead you and your lover to greater emotional magnetism.

Sexual Response and Long-Lasting Lovemaking

A common sexual concern for men and women is how to achieve a complete sexual response in order to enjoy lovemaking fully. We have been discussing that the Tao states that harmonizing Yin and Yang between partners is the most important aspect of experiencing strong arousal and long-lasting, fulfilling Sacred Love-Making. In addition, the health and vitality of our physical bodies inform our sexual response, as described in one of the ancient Taoist tomes entitled *The Classic of the Arcane Maid.* In it, one of the Immortal sisters, the Arcane Maid, gives a description of the male's "Four Attainments" and the female's "Nine Essences." This passage derived from this classic appears in the book *The Yin-Yang Butterfly.*

When a man has achieved his Four Attainments, only then can he bring the woman to her Nine Essences. "If the jade stalk is not angry, [in other words, aroused], his harmonious essence has not arrived. If it is angry but not large, his muscle essence has not arrived. If it is large but not rigid, his bone essence has not arrived. If it is rigid but not hot, his spirit essence has not arrived." These four physical attainments of an erect male penis are needed to enjoy a satisfying and lasting sexual experience.

"When the woman sighs deeply and swallows her saliva, her lung essence has been aroused. When she utters little cries and sucks his mouth, her heart essence has been aroused. When she enfolds and clings to him, her spleen essence has been aroused. When her yin gate is slippery and damp, her kidney essence has been aroused. [When she nibbles at him], her bone essence has been aroused. When she hooks her legs around him, her sinew essence has been aroused. When she caresses his jade stalk, her blood essence has been aroused. When she fondles his nipples, her flesh essence has been aroused."

The ninth essence can refer to the liver essence as well as the overall harmony of all essences to create an ecstatic lovemaking experience. Reaching these nine essences assures a beneficial sexual experience, according to the book *Sexual Secrets: The Alchemy of Ecstasy.*

In contemporary terms, when our health is vibrant, the sexual organs respond to intimate stimulation and activity naturally and easily. If the health of the vital organs and immune system is weak, it is more difficult to have a healthy sexual response. Supporting your health with healthy foods and regular exercise, as well as increasing your sexual strength and sexual hormonal health, which I will describe next, will increase your ability to achieve the four attainments and nine essences.

Sexual Strength

The urogenital diaphragm is the area located at the base of the body that includes the distance between the genitals and the anus. This group of muscles is often called the sexual muscle, love muscles, or perineum point. The strength and tone of these sexual muscles can indicate the ease with which the genitals are aroused. Like any other muscular group in the body, if these muscles are not exercised, they will lose their tone and become less useful. However, we can learn to strengthen our urogenital muscles and heighten our ability to respond sexually. Daily practice of Sexual Toning, an exercise from Fit for Love, can develop your sexual strength for a healthier sexual response.

Sexual Toning Exercise

Important notes: Women, do not practice the toning exercises while menstruating. Men and women, do not practice if you have a urinary tract infection.

Purpose:

Toning the sexual muscles increases genital strength for greater potency and pleasure. Sexual Toning also develops the urogenital diaphragm, which supports the entire body cavity and the health of the sexual organs.

Practice:

- Come into a squat position, with your heels turned in slightly. Place your elbows between your knees. Bring your hands into prayer position.
- Notice the urogenital diaphragm, the area from the genitals to the anus at the base of your body. Also be aware of the pelvic diaphragm, the bowl-like cavity that contains the Sexual Palace.
- Begin to inhale and contract the small muscular area between the genitals and the anus, called the perineum or the love muscles.
- Exhale and relax the area.
- Inhale and squeeze the love muscles.
- Exhale and relax them.
- Repeat three to nine times.

Sexual Hormonal Health

Sexual hormones play a large role in sexual response. As we move through different stages of life from adolescence to young adulthood, to mature adulthood, and then to older adulthood, our sexual hormone levels change. Influences on the hormonal system can include age, weight, health, and emotional stress levels. Our sexual hormone levels will affect the strength of both female and male arousal, as well as the time it takes to become sexually aroused. The Butterfly exercise can enhance your sexual hormonal health and support you in achieving a strong sexual response.

Butterfly (Reproductive and Lymphatic Massage for Women and Men)

Purpose:

This Fit for Love exercise creates a healthy flow of sexual hormonal energy through the sexual region and breasts and clears the lymphatic glands located there.

Practice:

- Butterfly position: Lie down on a mat and bring the bottoms of your feet together, with your knees straight out to the side. Let your legs gently pulse up and down on the mat to open the pelvic diaphragm.

- Place the pinky-finger side of each of your hands on each side of the groin where the leg and torso meet. Massage back and forth with gentle vigor.

- Change to using only your fingertips, as if you were playing the piano along the edge of the crease of the groin.

- Now bring the fingertips down to the area along both sides of the genitals. Play the piano again with your fingertips just along the crease. This practice brings more blood circulation into this part of the genital area.

- Slow down and stop. Smile.

- Feel new sexual energy and vitality increasing.

Butterfly with Breast Massage (For Women and Men)

- Continue to pulse your legs in the butterfly position on the ground as you bring your hands up and cup the breasts. Make circles with your fingers toward the center between the breasts.

- As you continue to pulse your legs in the butterfly position, circle around the breasts thirty-six times. Feel yourself activating the nurturing energy in the breasts.

- Circle in the opposite direction nine times. This massage relaxes the breasts, balances the reproductive hormones, and activates sexual arousal.

- Rest the fingertips in the center of the breasts at the heart center. Feel the breast and heart energy merging.

Butterfly with Ovarian and Testicular Massage
Step One for Women:
Bring the hands to the ovaries, which you can locate by placing your thumbs on your navel and spreading and extending the fingers downward. Your index and pinky finger will lie at the level of the ovaries. Begin in the butterfly position and again pulse the legs. Gently massage the ovarian area.

Step One for Men:
Begin in the butterfly position and again pulse the legs. Place your hands on the testicles and gently massage.

Step Two for Both Men and Women:
Both women and men should continue to massage and pulse the legs for several minutes. Now lengthen the legs straight out to the floor and extend the arms down by your sides. Relax and feel your body floating and resting. Feel your sexual and reproductive energy becoming more healthy and vibrant. This exercise is great for enhancing overall sexual and hormonal health.

Sexual Sensation

Sexual sensitivity is our immediate connection with our sexual response. Our ability to experience sexual sensation and pleasure throughout our sexual organs is an effect of the energy, vitality, and blood flowing through our sexual nerve endings.

The positive flow of vitality and energy through the Sexual Palace—described in the methods of Sex as Sacred Artistry in Part One—increases sexual organ health and sexual hormones, which in turn increase our sexual arousal and receptivity to sensual pleasure. The pace at which we experience arousal is an indicator of our current level of sexual sensitivity.

Intense Sensitivity

Many individuals complain that they are too sensitive and have no idea what to do with their intense sexual feelings and urges. They are aroused easily and lose their ability to sustain arousal quickly. Examples of being too sensitive are premature ejaculation, sexual impulsiveness, and physical sexual pain.

Without the development of sexual artistry, women and men who are too sexually sensitive can act impulsively on their sexual urges and wind up in sexual situations prematurely. Utilizing the Circulating Sexual Energy skill described in Part One will help such individuals develop their sexual sensitivity for amazing Sacred Love-Making fulfillment.

Suggestions for Premature Ejaculation and Impotence

For Premature Ejaculation
When a man is too sexually sensitive, he can ejaculate prematurely. But with the development of the Sex as Sacred Artistry skills mentioned in Part One, he can tune in to his sexual sensations to regulate his arousal rate, which will help him truly enjoy Sacred Love-Making.

Suggestions to Develop Sexual Endurance:
1. Sexual Toning, page 190
2. Breath of Pleasure, page 65
3. Circulating Sexual Energy, page 69

For Impotence
If you are having a problem with impotence (the inability for a man's penis to become fully aroused or stay aroused), get a checkup with your doctor, or see an acupuncturist to determine how your physical energy is out of balance. If illness is ruled out, then utilize some of the following.

Tips for Impotency:

Mental Attitude: Sometimes the problems of premature ejaculation and impotence are more mental than physical.

1. Shift focus from your performance—how long it lasted and how much you didn't satisfy your partner—to how much more pleasure you and your partner are having at this exact moment.

2. Stay in the *now*.

Develop Penile Strength: These developmental exercises are very helpful in increasing penile strength and endurance:

1. Sexual Toning, page 190

2. Breath of Pleasure, page 65

Intimacy: Act in harmony with your partner to enjoy a stronger sexual response, as detailed in Part Two: The Talent of Loving Another.

1. Allow your heart to connect to your partner. Opening the heart can create incredible sexual stimulation and pleasure.

2. Delight in the arousal of your partner.

Foreplay: This lends itself to strong erections.

1. Allow ample time for pleasure-filled foreplay with your partner.

2. Ask your partner to touch and massage your penis. Direct touch can help you to become erect, and this need increases as a man gets older. Focusing on your partner's pleasure can greatly help your own arousal.

Lovemaking: Some men can get aroused but then lose their arousal as they are about to make love or even during lovemaking. If this happens, you can:

1. Connect to your lover by looking into your lover's eyes and connecting heart to heart.

2. Focus on the love you have for your partner.

3. Try a soft entry. Once inside, begin to move (movement inside your partner can often stimulate the penis and create a strong erection).

4. Make a ring around your penis with your thumb and index finger or ask your lover to do this. Keep the ring around the penis as you begin to stroke, until you feel yourself growing hard inside.

5. Act leisurely, evenly, and gradually throughout your foreplay and lovemaking to sustain a strong erection.

Suggestions for Frigidity

Frigidity is caused by what Taoists call a "cold womb." A woman can warm the uterus by attending to underlying energies. When a woman's vagina lacks lubrication prior to having sex, it means that she is suffering from a kidney Yin, or water deficiency. When her vagina does not dilate, this is known as a deficiency in kidney Yang, or sexual desire. The kidneys are associated with the emotion of fear. Frigidity, like impotence, can be caused by either an emotional, physical, or atmospheric imbalance, or a combination of all three. This condition can cause a woman to feel indifference toward or have a lack of desire for sexual relations.

Tips for Frigidity:

Attitude: Your emotional outlook is important to becoming sexually aroused for lovemaking.
1. Address emotions around sexuality to feel more receptive to sexual pleasure.
2. Make sure you feel good about sharing yourself sexually with your lover.

Harmony: Emotional Harmony—addressed in Part One, Skill One—and Relationship Harmony—addressed in Part Two—are both equally important in having healthy sexual desire and female lubrication.
1. Spend time harmonizing with your partner daily.
2. Make sure both your heart and your partner's heart are open to love.
3. Focus on your heart softening and look lovingly into your partner's eyes to enhance receptiveness.

Heal Sexual Trauma: The following exercises can help women to heal past sexual trauma and increase their sexual desire, sensitivity, and vaginal secretions:
1. Sexual Toning, page 190
2. Butterfly, page 191
3. Breath of Pleasure, page 65
4. Reflexology Massage, page 211

Foreplay: This is key to greater lubrication and receptivity. Both partners need foreplay to relax into the sacred moment and open up to each other.

1. Make sure that you receive from your partner and give to your partner *satisfactory* foreplay.

2. Make foreplay a complete Sacred Love experience all by itself.

Lovemaking: If you find yourself feeling vaginal dryness during lovemaking:

1. Allow yourself to relax.

2. You can ask your partner to slow down or stop for a moment and then gently move again. Sometimes smaller, slower movements or none at all can ignite the fluids again.

3. Apply a lubricant, such as K-Y gel.

4. Position yourself on top of your lover to control the movement and the pace of love-making. This can also open the flow of sexual fluids.

5. Be aware of how your body responds to different movements. Rough sex or a sexual position that is uncomfortable for you can cause pain and fear, making a woman's body contract and her vaginal fluids dry up.

Impotence and frigidity can be healed when the emotional and the sexual experience are in harmony within each individual and between both partners. If you have suffered from impotence or frigidity challenges, explore how the suggestions above can transform your sex life into a more fulfilling experience for both you and your loved one.

Overcoming Being Tired

Do you want to connect sexually but find yourself feeling that you don't have the energy?

Most people feel lots of energy and enthusiasm for sex during the initial part of the relationship, but then find their interest or energy fading within three years into the relationship. As the natural sexual passion and magnetism between lovers starts to neutralize, couples can often feel their human fatigue, personal stresses, and unending day-to-day task lists taking precedence over sex.

Resting is very important to desiring and enjoying sex again. Your rest time can be part of the overall Sacred Love-Making experience. Let your rest awaken your energy and enthusiasm for connecting with your partner again. Schedule adequate rest time prior to Sacred Love-Making, either the night before or an hour before you begin lovemaking.

Here are some ideas for resting:

- Resting together in preparation for Sacred Love-Making is a great way to sexually synchronize and reenergize together.
- You can take a nap or meditate during your resting time.
- You can also rest in each other's arms after you complete a Sacred Love-Making experience.
- Try the next practice, below.

Sexual Meditation for Two

If you would like to connect sexually with your lover but are not up for full intercourse, try uniting in sexual meditation.

Take the performance out of sex by entering your partner without copulating. First, stimulate yourselves enough to unite the sexual organs and look into each other's eyes. Smile at your partner. Open your heart to your partner and enjoy your partner's sexual energy merging with your own. Meditate in silence. Recognize the divine essence and love in the face of your lover.

You may desire to move slowly to keep your sexual organs stimulated. You can also synchronize your breathing to deepen your connection.

Feel sexually nourished in the arms of your lover and appreciate this special and relaxing moment. Feel your unified sexual and heart energy connecting you in love. This meditation only takes a few minutes, leaving you refreshed and relaxed. You can wake up from a night's sleep, take a break in the afternoon or evening, or enter into a peaceful sleep afterwards by using this sexual merging meditation.

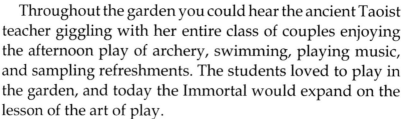

Throughout the garden you could hear the ancient Taoist teacher giggling with her entire class of couples enjoying the afternoon play of archery, swimming, playing music, and sampling refreshments. The students loved to play in the garden, and today the Immortal would expand on the lesson of the art of play.

"It is important to laugh and forget your lessons," she would always say. "Discipline combined with letting go will help you become a more natural lover."

The Immortal instructed one of her male students to play a lute, as he was finely skilled on such an instrument. She encouraged the class to watch as his fingers plucked delicately and then strongly across the strings. He played with passion, arousing a sweet harmony from his dedicated caresses.

When he was reaching a captivating crescendo in the music, the teacher spoke. "Only after extended play should intercourse begin." The students laughed heartily. When the students had quieted, the Immortal continued.

"Play connects us to our carefree, spontaneous self. Play easily lightens the heart and opens the body to enjoy pleasure. Play also connects us with the magical realm.

"Foreplay can take many forms in Sacred Love-Making. It can contain humorous laughter, deep erotic touch and kissing, spirited movement, and penetrating stillness.

Foreplay can act as a primer to lovemaking or perhaps become the entire lovemaking experience, providing the heights of orgasmic pleasure and spiritual bonding. Foreplay increases openness, excitement, and relaxation for a couple. Foreplay can also add healthy variation to the lovemaking experience."

"I have a hard time feeling comfortable letting go in foreplay in my new intimate relationship, teacher," said a concerned female student.

The Immortal responded, "It is natural that a foundation of trust and safety frees a couple to explore the full spectrum of play with one another. As your relationship develops, it is easier to let go into foreplay. Anxiety to reach a climatic moment becomes secondary to the overall fulfillment of the experience."

"What if I have little patience for foreplay?" asked a male student.

"Leaving out foreplay does not give partners ample time to harmonize and become sufficiently aroused. An absence of play often reduces lovemaking to routine intercourse. Both men and women can have challenges becoming fully aroused without foreplay. The time taken for foreplay can be adjusted for each lovemaking experience.

"Fulfilling foreplay for both partners ripens sexual response and generates satisfying and lasting lovemaking."

Art 3: Love Play

Play connects us to our most carefree and spontaneous selves. Here you will learn how to lighten your heart and open your body to full pleasure through laughter, erotic touch, passionate kissing—even spirited silliness! This primer for love heightens the entire lovemaking experience. Discover the Arts of Love Play such as: The Art of Playing, Dancing, and Laughing; The Art of Serving; The Art of Yin and Yang Foreplay; The Art of Sexual Reflexology; and The Art of Tongue Kung Fu.

The Art of Playing, Dancing, and Laughing

I want you to laugh
to kill all your worries
to love you
to nourish you
        —Rumi

Spontaneous Play

Spontaneous play, such as teasing, pillow fights, and a game of tag can be a great way to awaken your and your partner's passion. Find your playful side and use your imagination to bring lightness into your foreplay.

Dance

One of the best forms of erotic play I know is dancing. Create your own space for sacred dance in your home. All of us like to experience sensuality and sexual stimulation through our senses. Light some candles and turn on some beautiful, sexy music, perhaps with deep drumming and exotic rhythms. These kinds of sounds organically connect us into our pelvic area, which is the home of our sexual energy. Let your body come alive, and dance with your partner in a passionate way.

Allow the music to move through your body and ignite your passion. Celebrate your love through slow and fast rhythms, bringing your bodies close together. Drink in the attributes and features that attract you to your partner. Feel each other's skin, shape, and sexual arousal.

Meet each other eye to eye. Experience your souls and hearts uniting and delighting …

Dance Turns

You may want to take turns dancing for each other to show your partner your desire and your erotic rhythm. Try some moves that you always wanted to try and never have. Ignite your and your partner's passion with a sensuous, erotic dance just for the two of you.

Laughing

As you begin to let your mind and body go with play and liberate your passion with dance, you will feel more relaxed and happy. You can bring this joy into your lovemaking with laughter. Laughter takes lovemaking to a new level of play and pleasure. Allow your heart to open, and let the laughter flow out. Enjoy laughing together until you are giggling hysterically. Allow your laughter to open your and your partner's sexual enjoyment valves.

The Art of Serving

Sacred Love-Making is about great service—service to each other, service to your love, service to the sacred. The quality of your attention while giving, guiding, and satisfying your lover's needs for love and sexual fulfillment and making the moment meaningful communicates the refinement of your service capabilities.

Serving may seem like a forgotten art. Many people begin the act of lovemaking thinking about what is in it for them and how fast they can reach a desired destination. Serving can be watered down to just a few finger strokes on the clitoris or penis as the entire service portion of the lovemaking experience. While this is sometimes appropriate in the context of a quick, hot lovemaking session, resorting to the tiniest amount of service to your partner on a regular basis can effect the arousal, enjoyment, and overall benefits of your lovemaking experiences.

You Can Serve Your Lover By:

- Utilizing finesse and sensitivity in your touch
- Communicating love in your speech
- Being creative and poetic
- Electrifying your partner's passion by tuning in to his or her desires and pleasure
- Taking your time
- Remaining present

The Art of Yin and Yang Foreplay

Many intimate couples complain that routine sex diminishes their sexual desire. Usually this occurs when couples forget to play and have fun. You can experience more passionate excitement with your partner when you bring fun into your love life with a variety of foreplay techniques.

Yin Foreplay

Yin foreplay focuses on doing less and being more present and available to your partner and the moment. Yin foreplay encourages rest and organic flow. In this form of foreplay, the body is fundamentally stable and still.

If you have been overly productive and active before lovemaking and feel exhausted or stressed, then this is the foreplay for you. This foreplay relaxes your body and mind, allowing your natural, sensual flow to emerge. Take your time, rest, and caress each other. Connect with easy, fluid playfulness for lovemaking.

Yin Foreplay One: Taking the Waters

Purpose:
Relax and rejuvenate your mind and body for lovemaking. If you are especially stressed out or tired, add the water element to your foreplay experience to restore and revitalize.

Practice:
- Submerge yourself into a warm bath or a Jacuzzi to relax your muscles and let go of thoughts from the day.
- Add some of your favorites: bubble bath, bath salts, rose petals, candles, music, and serve chocolate-dipped strawberries to intensify your bathing experience.
- Venture out and go swimming with your lover in a pool or in the ocean under the moon-light. Bring along a blanket, and make love under the stars.

However you choose to soak up the waters with your lover, allow the experience to relax and rejuvenate you as you enjoy the moment of Sacred Love-Making.

Yin Foreplay Two: Erotic Poetry

Purpose:

Reading an erotic poem to your lover is a wonderful and easy way to awaken each other to the experience of lovemaking. In a relaxed and restful state, you can recite to each other words of passion and love.

Practice:

- While lying upon pillows in your sacred space, read one of your favorite poet's works to your lover.
- You can also write and recite your own inspired words about your feelings for your lover.
- Erotic, meaningful prose stimulates mental, emotional, and physical excitement for greater passion to be shared.
- Add this poetic element of romance to your foreplay experience.

Examples of Erotic Poetry:

Yes, the pulses were becoming very strong
Yes, the beating became very delicate
Yes, the calling ... the arousal
Yes, the arriving ... the coming
Yes, there it was for both entire
Yes, we were looking at each other
   From "Looking at Each Other"
   —Muriel Rukeyser

Show me your face I crave flowers and gardens
Open your lips I crave the taste of honey
   From "Show Me Your Face"
   —Rumi

How fair is thy love, my sister, my spouse! How much better is thy love than wine! and the smell of thine ointments than all spices! Thy lips, O my spouse, drop as the honeycomb: honey and milk are under thy tongue.
—Song of Solomon 4:10-11

Yin Foreplay Three: Intimate Touch with No Goals

Sharing intimate affection and touch without the goal of lovemaking adds a sexually receptive dimension, especially for the female lover or a male lover who needs rejuvenation.

Yang Foreplay

Yang foreplay ignites the fire for Sacred Love-Making. It encourages active physical and emotional expression. Yang generates vitality and an arousing drive for intimacy.

If you have been inactive, or too relaxed, this foreplay will add excitement and will intensify magnetic polarity between you and your lover. Stimulate, tease, and express your passion with your hands, fingers, and tongue to ignite the heat for lovemaking!

Yang Foreplay One: Foreplay Body Caress

A sensitive touch enhances your health and well-being and can bring out your sensual vitality and desire. Through a caring touch, you can massage tension and resistant emotions out of your lover's body. But a sensual touch activates hormones in the skin that can relax and arouse our bodies sexually. This type of sensual massage releases Yang energy flow in the body in a loving and sexually arousing way. It also releases the sexual and reproductive hormones found in the breasts and body that activate sexual stimulation and lubrication. This massage is equally pleasurable for both women and men.

Practice:
Choose one partner to give and the other to receive.

As the masseur/se:
- Apply a lotion or oil to the breast area of your partner.
- Place your hands on your partner's breasts, cupping them from underneath.
- Make gentle circles in toward the center between the breasts.
- Then circle up and over the breasts.

- Continue in this way, sending nurturing love to your lover's breasts.
- Then slowly caress up and down the sides and front of your partner's abdomen.
- Progress down between the thighs, then back toward the hips, and, if your lover desires, around to the clitoris, vagina, penis, or testicles. Caress and nurture your partner with this sexy foreplay massage as long as you both desire.

As the Receiver:

- Feel nurturing love building in the breasts and flowing down the body to the genital area, stimulating sexual arousal.
- Relax and enjoy this moment that is just for you.

Once the first foreplay body caress is completed, you can either change roles or proceed into making love if both partners are equally aroused.

Yang Foreplay Two: Take Charge

Purpose:
Initiate a foreplay experience with your lover. Approach your lover with a luscious love play activity you know he or she would like.

Practice:
Come up from behind your lover and kiss the back of their neck. Slowly undress your lover, teasing with the time you take and the sensuality of your touch. Keep your lover in a state of anticipation: you decide what you are going to do next. Perhaps lead your lover to the couch or bedroom and feed him or her a delicious selection of sumptuous fruits, or discover your lover's body with your tongue. There is something very erotic in this experience for a lover. This will ignite your sexual passion.

The Art of Sexual Reflexology

Discovery! Both women and men have more than one erogenous zone. Named after German gynecologist Ernst Gräfenberg, the G-spot is known as a highly erogenous zone found inside the vagina that can activate female orgasms. But besides the clitoris and the G-spot for women, and the highly sensitive head of the penis zone for men, there are other specific areas that enjoy pleasurable stimulation during sexual activity. These erogenous zones are called sexual reflexology points.

Like the feet and hands, the sexual organs have areas that are connected to different energy meridians that flow from the sexual area throughout the whole body. The penis and the inner walls of the vagina are the locations of a handful of reflexology zones that correspond to specific organs in the body. When a sexual reflexology zone along the penis or inside the vagina is stimulated, energy is directed to the corresponding part of the body, and great sexual pleasure can be felt there. These pleasure points are reflections of where our body desires, enjoys, and needs more energy flow. For instance, we can feel blissful sensations when a specific sexual position stimulates an organ that is in need of attention and revitalization.

All of our organs benefit from sexual stimulation. However, different organs may desire greater attention at different times. You will be able to identify which organs enjoy specific stimulation by referring to the following Sexual Reflexology Zones.

Reflexology Zones

You can explore your partner's pleasure spots and become aware of which organs they correspond to. These charts will prepare you for the following Sexual Reflexology Massage.

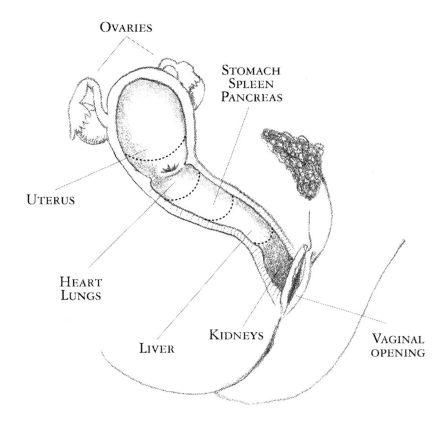

FEMALE REFLEXOLOGY

Women:

Kidneys: The opening of the vagina

Liver: The mid-section of the inside of the vagina

Spleen, Pancreas and Stomach: Past the mid-section into the vagina

Heart and Lungs: The back of the vagina

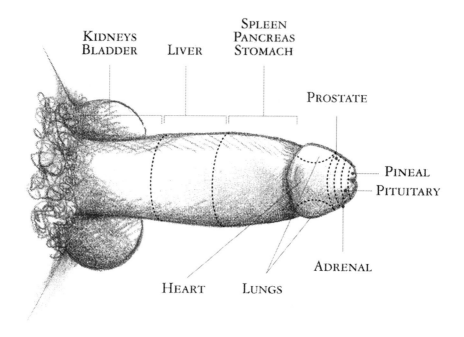

MALE REFLEXOLOGY

Men:
 Kidneys and Bladder: The base of the penis
 Liver: The mid-section of the penis
 Spleen, Pancreas and Stomach: Moving forward toward the top of the penis
 Lungs: Each far side of the head of the penis
 Heart: The center of the head of the penis
 Prostate gland, Adrenal and Thymus glands, Pituitary gland, and Pineal gland: These tiny individual zones are contacted on the top third section of the head of the penis.

While making love, the sexual reflexology points of the female and male sexual organs naturally touch each other at the same time. This stimulates both partners simultaneously in the same areas of the body.

Reflexology Massage
The following sexual reflexology massage is an arousing love-play treat as well as a health and energy tonic to enjoy with your lover.

As the masseur/se:
- Always make sure your fingernails are trimmed and clean, as the genital tissue is *very* sensitive.
- Smile to the genitals and apply a favorite lubricant to your partner's sexual region.
- Slowly massage the penis and testicles or the entrance of the vagina, nourishing it with a slow caress.

Receiver:
For the partner receiving, feel this caress awakening your pleasure and nourishing your sexual organs.

Pleasure Reflexes For Him:
When giving a man a reflexology massage explore around the right side of the penis. Then explore the left side of the penis. Caress around the base of the penis. Then caress along the bottom side of the penis. Massage up and down along the mid area of the penis. Massage gently around the head of the penis.

If you are giving the massage, let your partner tell you which areas feel the most stimulating. Let the receiver guide you toward the areas that feel most pleasurable.

Pleasure Reflexes For Her:
This art gives the act of "fingering" a whole new meaning. When giving a woman the sexual reflexology massage, you will need to add saliva or a lubricant. Gently slide the index finger inside of her and slowly caress the floor (bottom part) of her vagina in a half-circle motion. Slowly let the half-circle motion move up the left side of the vagina. Then move up the right side of the vagina. Ease back to the floor. Then make the half-circle motion at the top of the vagina. Now, move the finger further back in the vagina as far as the woman feels comfortable and continue to make circular motions.

This sacred massage for both men and women increases health and circulation in the genital area. Vital organs and the endocrine system are also stimulated to function more effectively.

The Immortal was lounging alone in the garden enjoying a mango when the couple that had spent their afternoon in the bedchamber behind the waterfall approached. From their appearances, the teacher knew their practice was going well. And she had more in store.

After savoring a last slice of juicy mango, the Immortal spoke. "Tongue Kung Fu is a play of the heart and tongue. Taoist love masters consider the tongue an extension of the heart. How one utilizes one's tongue with one's lover is a reflection of the heart connection to them. If one's words are kind, loving, and honorable, then tongue kisses will most often be long and deep. If one's words are critical and disrespectful, then tongue kisses are relatively short, as the heart is not fully open to the partner.

"When you give your lover your tongue, you give them your heart, igniting both lovers' passion. If both lovers' hearts are equally open to each other, their Tongue Kung Fu can electrify the body, heart, and spirit."

"What if my heart is open, but I feel uncomfortable giving Tongue Kung Fu?" asked the female student.

"First, you must discover what you are uncomfortable with and why. The discomfort of giving Tongue Kung Fu may arise from self-consciousness of expressing yourself in this erotic way. One who has suffered from sexual trauma may have difficulty expressing Tongue Kung Fu, as it can bring up memories of the trauma. In other cases, the sexual chemistry is not correct between you and the person your heart is open to. These experiences can inhibit Tongue Kung Fu from taking place. Acknowledging the reasons behind one's resistance is the first step, and then the reasons will need to be addressed appropriately."

"How can I become more skilled at Tongue Kung Fu?" asked the male student.

Suddenly, a sumptuous peeled and cored peach appeared, dangling in front of the male student's face. And then a ripe banana appeared in front of the female student.

"Tongue Kung Fu involves the skillful combination of utilizing the tongue, lips, teeth, and intention," said the love master. "This oral love-play practice can increase your skill and ability to give and enjoy incredible pleasure and stimulate arousal for Sacred Love-Making."

The love Immortal gestured to her students to practice this play without consuming their delicious fruit before they headed back to the private sanctuary behind the waterfall to express their new artistry.

The Art of Tongue Kung Fu

In the Chinese Taoist tradition, the tongue is the outer organ connected to the heart. Nature's element of fire governs the heart, and the heart in turn rules over the tongue. The quality of our fire nature represents our enthusiasm for life.

We can see the connection of the heart and tongue by how we speak to our lover. The tone and words we use are a clear indication of what is happening in our heart. In addition, the way we use our tongue in kissing our lover expresses our level of fiery feelings about connecting to him or her emotionally as well as sexually.

Giving and receiving love and pleasure orally is a way to genuinely wake up the heart as well as sexual desire. Some people may feel self-conscious receiving or giving kisses or oral sex. If this is true for you, talk with your partner about the reasons why you feel this way, and see if the resistance can be resolved.

Kissing

Kissing is a primary skill of a Tongue Kung Fu artisan and can be two lovers' favorite pastime. When we feel attraction to someone, we long to kiss. We kiss to express our passion—and the *way* we kiss says a lot about our emotional and sexual feelings toward our lover.

Kissing Quiz
Take this quiz to find out who you are as a kisser.

1. How do you feel about kissing?
   A. I love to kiss
   B. I love to be kissed
   C. I like to kiss
   D. I think kissing is okay
   E. I don't like to kiss at all

2. When do you feel like kissing?
   A. When I'm sexually attracted
   B. When I'm in love
   C. When my lover and I are harmonious
   D. Anytime

    E. Only in the lead-up to or during sex

3. How do you kiss?

    A. I kiss passionately

    B. I French kiss

    C. I make out for long periods of time

    D. I kiss all over the body

    E. I kiss on the mouth

    F. I kiss on the cheek

    G. I give oral sex

    H. I don't know how to kiss

4. How do you like to use your tongue?

    A. I play with my lover's tongue in deep, hot kisses

    B. I practice creative moves with my tongue to awaken my lover's heart and body

    C. I like giving oral sex

    D. I use my tongue gently

    E. I use my tongue with strength

    F. I do not like tongue kissing, it seems invasive

5. In what stages of relationship do you love to kiss passionately?

    A. When I first meet my lover

    B. Throughout dating my lover

    C. When we have officially taken the next stage of couplehood (marriage or living together)

    D. At every stage of the relationship

The scoring of your quiz is up to you! You can discuss the results with your lover and practice the following Tongue Kung Fu techniques to expand your kissing repertoire.

The Taste of Ambrosia

Your partner should taste like ambrosia to you. Ambrosia, known as the food of the gods, is a pleasing and satisfying taste and scent. The natural scent and taste of your partner are good indicators of whether you and your partner are sexually compatible. Your partner's saliva, sexual scents, and fluids should be compelling and enjoyable to you. This chemical factor has been the subject of several scientific studies about conceiving healthy offspring. A February 2006 *National Geographic* article titled "This Thing Called Love" details a study by Claus Wedekind at the University of Lausanne in Switzerland. Wedekind had forty-nine women smell T-shirts that had been worn by unidentified men. He asked the women to rate them from best to worst smelling. What he found was that the women liked the scents that were most different from their own. He concluded that this difference in scent might have indicated an immune system that possessed something the women's did not, which could increase the chance that offspring with the different-smelling men would be healthy.

In other words, this study indicates that if you like each other's scents, you are more likely to have healthy offspring. If you do not, you may want to address the factors of diet, hygiene, and exercise to improve the compatibility of your physical scents and tastes.

Tasting and Embodying Ambrosia

The more the taster sinks into the experience of giving oral pleasure, the easier it is to awaken your lover's pleasure as well as your own. Giving oral pleasure in the Taoist tradition is compared to drinking from the fountain of youth, as the sexual secretions of both lovers are said to carry vital, life-giving properties. The lovers can achieve rejuvenation and gratifying orgasms. The intense stimulation and pleasure your partner receives will add fuel to the flames of your passion.

Tasting Ambrosia

A Tongue Kung Fu master's skill for giving is determined by:

1. The joy and reverence of their giving
2. The level of sensitivity the giver has to his or her partner's experience of pleasure
3. Creativity and fun
4. Perceptiveness of both how and how long to deliver specific types of pleasure to their partner's erotic zones
5. Adding hot sensual movements with the body while giving Tongue Kung Fu

Allowing yourself to embody ambrosia, the essence of sweet and sacred nectar, will help you let go of anxiety about oral sex and will bring you the gifts of feeling love, arousal, rejuvenation, pleasure and even gratifying orgasms. The more you sink into embodying ambrosia and receiving oral pleasure, the easier the sexual, emotional, and spiritual energies can be activated within you to experience incredible pleasure. The intense stimulation that you receive from your lover will ignite your desire for more romance and passion.

Embodying Ambrosia

To receive Tongue Kung Fu skillfully, you must:

1. Be willing to trust, open, and receive
2. Surrender to the pleasure, sensuality, and fire between you and your partner
3. Stay present with the pleasure
4. Keep your mind on the sensations that the body is experiencing in the moment
5. Feel this as a meditation and gift from your lover

Tongue Play

The tongue is the greatest of arousers. Tongue play can begin with kissing your lover's mouth passionately, utilizing sensitivity and a variety of tongue movements.

Passionate Mouth-to-Mouth Kissing is Best When You:

*   Meet your lover's lips at an angle and then adjust in various directions.
*   Feel and enjoy the flesh of your lover's lips by gently pressing against each other's lips before giving them your tongue. This is *very* arousing.
*   Slide your tongue inside your lover's mouth to meet your lover's tongue.
*   Allow your tongues to playfully spar, nibble, and the lips to suck each other's tongue. You can also throw in occasional nibbles on the mouth and face.

Remember: No limp tongues! No one likes a tongue that just lays limp in their mouth. Holding your mouth rigid on your lover's mouth and slobbering are also prohibited. No one enjoys a bad kiss.

Tongue and Body Play

If your lover and you desire, proceed to use your tongue as if it were a seductive "pleasure feather," exploring your lover's erotic body zones—the face, ears, breasts, underarms, sides of the torso, navel, shoulders, spine, hips, inner thighs, legs, ankles, and feet. Use your imagination as your tongue becomes a feather that gently contacts your lover to tickle and arouse sensation. You can use this tongue play for kissing the mouth and body as well as for giving oral sex.

Playful Tongue Flutters

The tongue can act as a vibrator; think of a hummingbird's wings on slow speed.

This fluttering movement is a rapid back-and-forth movement of the tongue that can be used in arousing the mouth, ears, underarms, abdomen, inner thighs, scrotum, clitoris, and vagina.

Licking

Licking can be very sexy. Use long, slow licks where the front tip of the tongue contacts the skin, and then the mid to back part of the tongue makes contact. Licking can be utilized around the breasts, along the body, along the length of the vagina or penis, around the scrotum, and along the division of the buttocks. Licking can send either lover into a super state of arousal.

Sucking

Use both lips, the tongue, and even the teeth to suck your lover's tongue, breasts, labia, penis, and scrotum—and, if you desire, the ankles, toes, and feet.

Biting

Biting is like nibbling. The delicate use of your teeth can be electrifying to your lover. Use gentle biting on the lips, tongue, ears, neck, body, penis, and inner thighs.

Tongue Diving

Tongue diving is the straightest, strongest use of your tongue to reach deep into the vagina for titillating oral intercourse.

Scooping the Tongue

Here the tongue is utilized in a come-hither motion for exploring the treasures of your lover's mouth during kissing. You can also utilize this tongue movement to arouse a man's penis and perineum point as well as a woman's G-spot (located on the front, also called top, wall inside the vagina, about three inches from the opening). Roll the first third of your tongue upwards in a curled position, touching the roof of your lover's mouth, G-spot, or around the penis. Use the scooping motion in combination with the others mentioned to arouse and stimulate your lover orally.

Fellatio and Cunnilingus

Once your lover has relaxed into oral ecstasy, continue with fellatio (oral sex performed on the penis) or cunnilingus (oral sex performed on the vagina). Utilize the following tongue artistry techniques to arouse and satisfy your lover.

A Cunnilingus Play

Women respond to oral sex that contains sensitivity and strength. Use your tongue as if it were a penis. Gently contact the clitoris. Utilize the pleasure feather technique to stimulate the clitoris in an up-and-down as well as a circular motion. Not all clitorises are visible, so you may need to fold the lips of the vagina back with your fingers to reach the clitoris. In some cases, it still may not be visible under the hood. If this is the case, then the entire hood should be stimulated to excite the invisible clitoris underneath.

The clitoris also responds to long licks and gentle fingering. Sucking the lips of the vagina is very stimulating to a woman. Put one or both of the lips inside your mouth, and suck with both strength and gentleness. Then guide your tongue into the vagina and explore the sides, top, and bottom with playful flutters. Try deep and shallow thrusts with the tongue-diving technique. Don't forget to stimulate the G-spot with the tongue-scooping technique to bring your lady lover wonderful sexual pleasure!

A Fellatio Play

Men respond very well to delicate and passionate fellatio that is combined with hand stimulation. Use your mouth like a vagina to mount the penis. Glide your mouth up and down the shaft of the penis. You may want to begin with a deep throat kiss, bringing your mouth all the way to the base of the penis and then softly gripping it with your mouth as you glide your mouth back to the top. Use your tongue to lick the head of the penis or graze your lips across it. Use your whole mouth to just suck the head while gliding the tongue delicately along the crease of the back of the head.

Use your hand, preferably with saliva, but a lubricant can also be used, to stimulate the rest of the penis while your lips are on the head. Vary hand strokes from fast to slow. You can also massage the testicles and perineum point (found underneath the scrotum and before the anus) to stimulate the prostate gland—a male G-spot. Use your intuition and your lover's responses to guide you through an arousing fellatio play.

Sharing Ambrosia or 69 Position

Mouth-to-genital stimulation given simultaneously is what Westerners have nicknamed 69. I like to call it "Sharing Ambrosia." When you and your lover give oral sexual pleasure to each other simultaneously, you are connecting to the Microcosmic Orbit that surrounds each person's body. In the Sharing Ambrosia position, one Microcosmic Orbit forms through both lovers.

In this oral pleasure position, the Microcosmic Orbit creates a flow of energy from the mouth of the giver through the receiver's genitals and up the spine to the receiver's head. As the circuit reaches the top of the head (called the crown center), it ignites the energy of divine awareness. Then the energy travels through the mouth of the receiver. The energy continues down the front of the receiver's body to their genitals, where the sexual energy is exchanged again with the giver to continue the circulation of the orbit.

Couples find that they can easily orgasm and enjoy ecstasy as the natural Microcosmic Orbit begins to open in this foreplay position. Sharing Ambrosia can be a complete sexual experience. This incredible Tongue Kung Fu practice unites the tongue and heart energy with the sexual organs to increase sexual, emotional, and spiritual pleasure.

It is possible to experience ecstatic orgasms during any form of Tongue Kung Fu. Enjoy the beautiful moments of sacred pleasure that you can create with your mouth and tongue!

The Immortal continued with her stories, again supporting the couple on their Sacred Love-Making journey in the sanctuary.

"The Yellow Emperor of China once asked me, 'Why do some feel uncomfortable around sexuality?'"

The Immortal became silent so the couple could think about this. Then she answered, "Confusion."

"Love masters acknowledge that the expression of sexuality is natural and beautiful. Sexual expression utilized appropriately is a positive human activity. With this awareness, ease with our bodies and the experience of sensual enjoyment deepens. It inspires us to fluidly dance with and celebrate our sexual essence.

"Animals possess a natural, sensual, and erotic beauty. Our own sexuality shares similarities with certain movements of wild animals. Many Taoist lovemaking positions are named after exotic creatures. Each movement expresses an aspect of our own wild, sexual nature. As we express our sexuality with a wild, natural passion, authenticity, and joy, we can provide nourishment to our lover and ourselves for an overall healthy lifestyle."

The couple looked at each other, intrigued …

Art 4: Wild and Sacred Positions

The Tao acknowledges the many variants that make sexuality natural and beautiful. With that awareness, this chapter will provide artistry for you to learn how to become at ease with your body and invite the deepening of your own sensuality. You will learn to dance with your own sexual essence by exploring sacred sexual positions. In this chapter, you will discover Sex in Nature, Making Love in the Earthly Garden, Making Love at Dawn and Dusk, Integrating the Primal, as well as Wild and Sacred Animal Positions.

Sex in Nature

Nature is exquisitely sensual. In the scents of flowers, the ocean, and forest, in the colors of vegetation, in the shapes of rock formations, the curves of mountain ridges, and the temperatures of seasons, the pulsing vibration of sexuality is alive.

When we enter nature, we can attune to this primal play bursting with life. We can allow the scents, sounds, and images to filter into our consciousness and bodies and enter our hearts.

I love the feel of the intense heat and the sensuousness of vegetation in the late summer that makes my body pulsate. Palm trees, balmy nights, the scent of salt air and the sensation of warm wind on my face can always arouse me and bring my love of nature to new heights.

Think about what arouses you in nature:
- Trees (What kind?)
- Flowers (What kind?)
- Season (Which one?)
- Beach (What kind?)
- Lake (Where?)
- Mountains (What kind?)
- Scents (Which ones?)
- Sounds (Which ones?)
- Time of day?

How do these different aspects of nature make you feel?
Do they make you feel sexually inspired?

Let them inspire your next sexual adventure with your lover.

Making Love in the Earthly Garden

The earth is an abundant erotic paradise. You can find the supple sexiness of nature in the beauty of any place or season. Take an outing with your lover into nature. Bring along a picnic, and make your fantasies of making love in the open air under the sun or moon come true.

Going for a Hike

- Bring along a blanket and some nice treats.
- Find a beautiful, isolated spot.
- Spend the afternoon or evening making love.
- Soak in the sensuousness of your surroundings with your lover.
- Listen to the sounds of nature: birds, bees, crickets, and any other animals that you may hear.
- Listen to the wind blowing.
- Harmonize your sighs of pleasure with the sounds of nature.
- Feel your lovemaking reach a new vibration.

Making Love against a Tree

- You may like to make out and make love while leaning against a tree with your lover.
- Allow the tree energy to support you.
- Feel the vibration of the tree pulsing and blending with you and your lover.
- You can also utilize the Sacred Love-Making techniques to circulate sexual energy for incredible effects in this position.
- As you orgasm, share your sensations with the nature that surrounds you. Nature will join in your celebration and share even more splendid natural energy with you.

If you would like to make love in a beautiful natural setting but feel it's a little too far from your home, try your own backyard (if you have one) and enjoy the erotic delights possible there. You will develop a whole new appreciation for the festivities you can enjoy just outside your door!

Sexual Sunbathing

The backyard is also a great place to have a little erotic sunbath on your genitals. Five minutes of sunning your genitals is incredibly nourishing. You can lie down with your legs spread facing the sun, or do a simple yoga shoulder-stand with the legs open and your hands supporting your hips. This can create nice stimulation of the genitals, which can be a great foreplay treat. Be mindful of not taking in too much sun; this is a sensitive area that you do not want to burn.

Making Love at Dawn and Dusk

Dawn and dusk are magic hours. We have all been awed by an amazing sunset and, if we are early risers, a beautiful sunrise. This is the case because something very special happens in nature at these two times of the day. As the sun comes up in the morning, chi—life force—rises. Yang, the day, has risen to kiss Yin, the night, and they unite for a magical moment before they go their separate ways. As the sun goes down in the evening, chi descends. Yin, the night, ascends to meet Yang, the day, and they embrace again in perfect harmony for another brilliant, magical moment. The celebration of their love for each other is seen in every beautiful sunset and sunrise.

Lovemaking at Dawn

As the light begins to rise in the morning sky, our energy also rises. Dawn is an ideal time to make sacred love with your partner. Yin and Yang's harmonic energy is naturally supportive for you to make love with your partner at this time. Play with the energy of the rising chi to increase your vital energy, have amazing sex, and amplify your loving vibration for the day.

Lovemaking at Dusk

As the sun sets, our bodies begin to relax and naturally unwind. At this time we may get a bolt of energy to have fun and socialize with others. This relaxing time is also an ideal time to make love. Let yourself dissolve into the sensations of letting go and opening up. Surrender to your lover like the setting sun does to the night.

Integrating the Primal

In the ancient Taoist tradition, animals were observed closely for their behaviors and movements. Certain animals' traits and qualities were copied by love sages to enhance different aspects of human health and well-being.

Animals that we are drawn to or feel we have an affinity with hold medicine for us. Native American traditions also share this Taoist belief. For instance, the deer is revered in Taoist tradition for its sexual skills and reproductive abilities. Taoist sages saw that the deer regularly exercised its anus when it wiggled its tail by contracting the anus and then relaxing it. The sages immediately adopted the principle and adapted it for human use, which is detailed in the method of using the Breath of Pleasure.

Like the deer, other animals were noted for their movements during coitus. Many times, we are naturally drawn to these animal positions to express a certain aspect of passion and feeling for our lover during the act of lovemaking.

People have often shunned and kept secret their primal animal nature, as it has long been thought to be a bad and beastly attribute. But our animal nature is in fact very empowering to our healthy self-expression. It can characterize and bring out different traits and strengths within us and support us in different areas at specific times in our lives.

Understanding the meaning of our natural magnetism toward specific animals and certain sexual movements can bring even more naturalness, acceptance, enjoyment, and pleasure to us during the act of lovemaking.

Let Out the Wild Animal in You

Acting like an animal can actually strengthen your sexual organs and help you understand the medicine that you need right now in your love life. Think of your favorite animal and why you are drawn to that animal. What characteristics do you identify with in your favorite animal? These characteristics would symbolize what the animal brings out in your personality.

Animal lovemaking positions work the same way. The ones you are most drawn to offer healing and pleasure benefits for you. Play and move with your partner like the animals you love. It also feels very good to try new positions. Try a powerful, seductive tiger, a slinky snake, a playful monkey, or a fun-loving panda bear. If you need some animal movement inspiration, then rent some nature videos to view and enjoy with your lover.

These wild and sacred animal positions can increase your and your lover's ecstatic pleasure, health, and sacred union. Allow the lovemaking positions to be organic and fluid, and enjoy the untamed moment. Bring your animal instincts out to increase your orgasmic joy.

Wild and Sacred Animal Positions

Try a new position—or bring new meaning to old favorites—with the following Taoist love artisan positions. These movements are said to remove one hundred ailments!

Note: I will be describing some compelling Taoist female-male lovemaking positions. Those who have a same-sex orientation can adjust the positions accordingly.

Also, in the following Taoist movement descriptions, you will see that the man chooses to retain his semen. This is because in the Taoist tradition, the loss of semen is a loss of vital energy, and love masters make every ejaculation a conscious one. Developing the ability to choose if and when to ejaculate in a lovemaking experience and how often ejaculation is beneficial to you is one of the fundamental skills that you can cultivate from learning these lovemaking arts described throughout the rest of Part Three.

Stepping Tigers
Unleash the Tiger Nature in You

The woman comes on to all fours, with her head down and her buttocks raised. The man penetrates her deeply from behind with short and long strokes of his penis. The man, in a kneeling position, holds the woman's stomach and continues his strokes until she emits her erotic juices. The woman contracts and expands her vagina until her vaginal fluids flow. The man retains his semen throughout the lovemaking encounter. This is a great position for stimulating the woman's G-spot.

Soaring Phoenix
Experience the Mystical State of Sacred Love

There are two variations for this position. In the first, the woman lies back and raises her legs. The man straddles her legs. His feet are flat on the bed beside her abdomen so that both lover's sex organs are facing each other and their buttocks are touching. In the second, the woman again lies on her back and raises her legs. The man kneels between her thighs and balances himself on the bed with his hands.

Once in position, the male moves rapidly, pressing against the female's buttocks. She moves toward him, opening and releasing her vaginal juices.

Wrestling Monkeys
Play in the Erotic Jungle of Desire

The woman lies face up. Her lover kneels and pushes her knees past her breasts, supporting her buttocks and back. His penetration is fast and rhythmic for ten to thirty seconds, then still. She amply emits her vaginal juices. The male does not ejaculate throughout the lovemaking experience.

Cleaving Cicadas
Climb the Tree of Living Ecstasy

The woman lies extended on her stomach. The man rests, stomach-side down, on her back. He raises her buttocks slightly with his hands to better reach her genital area. This position allows his penis to stimulate the lips of his lover's vagina and the clitoris. He may thrust shallow strokes around the entrance of the vagina and then deep strokes into the vagina, arousing his lover until she expands and contracts. He does not ejaculate.

Bunny Licking Its Fur
Enjoy Lovemaking Vitality and Longevity

The man lies on his back in a relaxed "Yin position," facing upwards. The woman turns around backward in a squatting position directly over his genitals, facing his legs. She lowers her head as she holds onto the bed and inserts his penis into her vagina. She makes shallow hops up and down on his penis, varying the rhythm between fast and slow in her Yang position. Thigh strength is important for her to be able to execute this position well. The man is relaxed in this Yin position until his partner's juices are aroused. He does not ejaculate.

Linking Dolphins
Swim in the Ocean of Sexual Bliss

This is another role-change position where the man takes the receptive Yin position and the woman takes the giving Yang position. The man lies on his back with the woman lying on top, facing him. She hugs his thighs with her own. This position allows the woman to move in a way that is pleasing to both her and her lover. She keeps the penetrations of his penis shallow and rocks back and forth and up and down. They rejoice in great pleasure.

Cranes Entwining
Infinite Pleasure and Love are Available in this Moment

The man comes into a squatting position. The woman straddles the man by wrapping both her legs around him. Her hands hold his neck. He clasps her buttocks to aid her mobility, and together they move slow or fast, and in an up, down, and spiraling motion. This position takes endurance and thigh strength from both parties to move in a way that is pleasing to both. Enjoy this ecstatic, erotic journey.

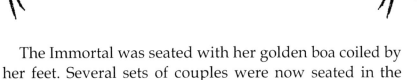

The Immortal was seated with her golden boa coiled by her feet. Several sets of couples were now seated in the garden with her.

"The sexual elixir was prehistoric China's quest for the Holy Grail," began the teacher.

"This elixir was greatly desired for its life-giving and ecstatic mystical properties.

"There were many who went in search of the secrets of the elixir during the reign of the Yellow Emperor, as his life and accomplishments were proof of their astounding workings.

"When the great female love master Sun Buer was sought out by an eager adventurer and asked how to learn the secret of the sexual elixir, she responded with this poetic cryptology, 'The elixir pill forms like a dew drop at the point where the womb breath is continuous. With every breath return to the beginning of the creative. The energy returns coursing through the three islands.'

"This coded terminology describes the ultimate arts of Sacred Love-Making," continued the Immortal.

"When a sincere couple comes together to make love, by understanding and practicing this secret skill they can co-create the sexual elixir and reap its treasures for intimate pleasure, health, well-being, and sacred bonding.

"Each of you has been cultivating your skills for this incredible experience. It is now time for you to engage with your lover, love artist to love artist, with all of your talents."

At that, the golden boa uncoiled and ascended the luscious fig tree, offering the Immortal a taste of the divine fruit.

Art 5: Sacred Love-Making and the Sexual Elixir

Believed to be the secret to immortality based on the immortal Yellow Emperor of China's practice of the sexual arts, the sexual elixir will inspire your own Sacred Love-Making. Here I have adapted this principle for modern times to help you and your lover create your own sexual elixir for ecstatic, meaningful, rejuvenating, and enlightened lovemaking. Now it is time for you to learn Lovemaking for Body and Soul, Making Love with Sexual Energy Circulation, Creating the Sexual Elixir, The Palace Odyssey, Moment-to-Moment Bliss, Partaking of the Sexual Elixir, Reaching Multi-Orgasmic Lovemaking, Sacred Love-Making, and finally, Surrendering to Ecstasy and Ultimate Love.

Lovemaking for Body and Soul

Sacred Love-Making is the ultimate sexual experience, as it is sex for your body *and* soul. It is this integral experience of sexual, emotional, mental, and spiritual intercourse with your lover that offers a new world of intimate sexual discovery.

Naked Body, Naked Soul

We enter the bedchamber with a naked body, and as a love artist, we also enter with a naked soul. Within the shared closeness of this event, our self acceptance, openness, appreciation, sensitivity, and art for serving our lover shine through. Standing in front of your lover with a naked soul is often much more intimidating than standing in front of your lover physically naked. If this is the case, allow your breathing to bring you more confidently and fully into the moment. An open body *and* soul can more readily enjoy and receive the wealth of possibilities available during the experience of Sacred Love-Making.

Sacred Love-Making with the sexual elixir provides the recipe for experiencing even fuller physical and emotional pleasure. In this way, lovers can achieve multiple orgasmic ecstasy as well as exalted sexual communion. Spiritual rapture can also be induced within the vessel of this meaningful lovemaking experience.

Sacred Love-Making utilizes the skills and talents that have come before in Part One: The Sacred Lover and Part Two: The Talent of Loving Another, as well as the arts in Part Three: The Art of Sacred Love-Making.

Making Love with Sexual Energy Circulation

A love artist cultivates and circulates sexual energy through the Microcosmic Orbit. This is the secret of sexual ecstasy, and it is the ultimate health and energy tonic.

The golden key to making love in this way is to be able to circulate your sexual energy while making love through the two major energy channels of the body that form the Microcosmic Orbit.

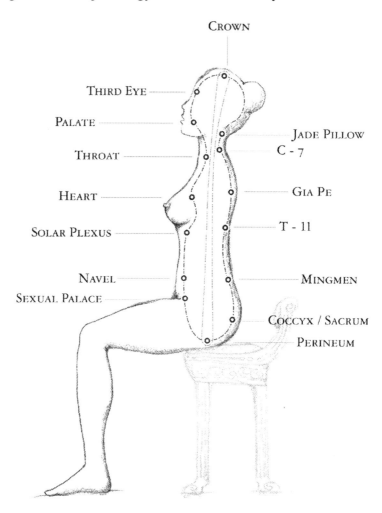

CROWN

THIRD EYE

PALATE

THROAT

HEART

SOLAR PLEXUS

NAVEL

SEXUAL PALACE

JADE PILLOW
C - 7

GIA PE

T - 11

MINGMEN

COCCYX / SACRUM

PERINEUM

MICROCOSMIC ORBIT

The orbit begins at the navel and flows down to the base of the body at the perineum, up the length of the spine to the crown of the head, down the center of the face through the upper palate of the mouth, and then continues back down toward the navel. The back spinal channel represents the individuals' Yang—fire or masculine energy—and the front channel represents the individuals' Yin—water or feminine energy. To learn how to move sexual energy fluidly and safely through the Microcosmic Orbit, practice on your own, as detailed in Sex as Sacred Artistry in Part One, prior to utilizing sexual energy circulation during lovemaking with your lover.

During Sacred Love-Making you will utilize the Breath of Pleasure and the Circulating Sexual Energy techniques depicted in depth in Sex as Sacred Artistry to generate the sexual elixir with your lover and then channel it through your body and throughout your partner's body. When you and your lover can generate the sexual arousal essences, the sexual elixir is manifested. Then the lover's elixir is sipped up into your cosmic orbits and released as a showering waterfall of ecstatic pleasure throughout both lovers' spiritual, emotional, and sexual palaces.

Sexual Energy Etiquette

Before beginning lovemaking with sexual circulation, it is important to respect sexual energy etiquette and safety precautions that will create more harmony, well-being, and fulfillment during the lovemaking encounter. It is also important to remember that this is a sacred skill that is designed for mutual benefit for *both* partners.

Etiquette Tips:

- When utilizing sexual energy circulation during lovemaking, let your partner know beforehand that you will be practicing these methods.
- If your partner is not aware of the practice, communicate and show your partner how the skill works so he or she can participate fully.
- Share the sexual elixir energy that you create with your lover equally during lovemaking.
- Do not become an "energy vampire" by taking in your partner's energy and not giving and sharing your own.

Tips for Women

- Do not practice Creating the Sexual Elixir when you are menstruating, as it can prevent the completion of your menstrual cycle.

- Women who practice Sexual Energy Circulation techniques daily will see a decline in the numbers of days and the severity of symptoms they experience during menstruation—or the menstrual cycle may even stop. This only happens with diligent practice on a long-term basis, usually for more than a year, with the intention to stop having a monthly menstrual cycle. If you stop your menstrual cycle and want it to return, stop practicing the techniques, and the menstrual cycle will start back up again.

Tips for Men

- As expressed earlier, make every ejaculation a conscious one. The following methods will help you develop your ability to choose if and when to ejaculate in a lovemaking experience and how often ejaculation is beneficial for you.

- These techniques will teach you how to separate orgasm from ejaculation by practicing sexual energy cultivation.

- If practiced regularly, you can decrease the number of ejaculations and increase the number of orgasms, resulting in experiencing multiple orgasms. This becomes more natural the more you practice the sexual cultivation techniques.

Safety Precautions for Women and Men

- Always bring the energy back to the dantien, the area below the navel, by circulating your hands there after lovemaking to prevent overheating, energy getting stuck in the head, and lightheadedness or nausea.

- Don't underestimate the power of your practice. These techniques can help you in all areas of life if you use them appropriately, but they can harm you and others if you use them inappropriately. For instance, if you have not refined your sexual energy with the use of the Creating the Sexual Elixir technique, your unrefined energy may not move properly and can get trapped in another area of the body. This can cause pain until you can circulate your energy back to the dantien. Energy-vampiring is also a harmful practice that can drain a partner's energy, leaving him or her depleted. Practicing these techniques in an unhealthy relationship can also be harmful to your overall well-being.

Creating the Sexual Elixir

Alchemists throughout history have sought to create an elixir that would prolong life and transform base materials into gold. Creating the sexual elixir is such a process. Both lovers gather the sexual essence at the base of their bodies and transform it into a refined, incredibly valuable substance. Creating the sexual elixir is essential for awakening, pleasuring, and rejuvenating your and your lover's body and soul.

The elixir can be perceived as juicy pleasure sensations tingling and rippling through your Sexual Palace. The elixir stimulates your sexual arousal. Tune in to the rich properties of the sexual elixir forming.

Creating the Sexual Elixir with the Breath of Pleasure

1. First join in coitus, and begin to make love.

2. Slowly breathe in and practice the Breath of Pleasure described here:
   Women: Inhale, and close the entrance of the vagina.
   Men: Inhale, and close the tip of the penis while drawing up the testicles.

3. Exhale.

4. Relax the contraction of the genitals.

5. Open up and fully relax.

6. Synchronize your breathing with your lover.

7. Repeat this breathing pattern three to six times.

Creating the sexual elixir will add great pleasure to your lovemaking experience. Make sure you feel relaxed and comfortable with the muscular movement of your genitals. This exercise is not meant to produce pain in any way. The genital movements should match your breathing patterns. Have fun synchronizing sexually with your lover through breathing, strengthening your arousal, and creating the sexual elixir.

The Palace Odyssey

A great deal of enjoyment during lovemaking arises out of both lovers' compatible erotic stroking and pelvic movements within the Sexual Palaces. What treasures await inside the Sexual Palace are a result of the male's penetration strength, sensitive stroking skills, and pelvic circulation, combined with the female's vaginal muscular strength, pelvic circulation, and sexual receptivity. Thigh strength and hip openness also support each lover in executing these lovemaking skills. These delicious movements create the sexual potion for incredibly satisfying lovemaking.

The following sexual stroking and pelvic movements can increase your and your lover's fulfillment during your sexual odyssey.

G-spot Stroking

The classic female G-spot, a highly erogenous zone found inside a woman's vagina, can activate female orgasms. It is part of the urethral sponge located midway between the pubic bone and the uterine wall. When stimulated, the G-spot can swell, offering very pleasurable sensations to the woman. With the right stimulation of the G-spot on the vagina's front wall, a woman can enjoy a satisfying orgasm and may even ejaculate clear fluid from the Skene's glands. It can be a little, a lot, or no fluid at all. A woman may initially feel self-conscious and wonder if she is urinating during sex. This is not the case. Female ejaculation is generally odorless and is a slightly thicker substance than urine.

Initially, you may want to use your tongue or finger in an inviting "come hither" stroking gesture to contact the G-spot during foreplay. Reach the tongue or finger one to three inches inside the vagina and then flitter the tongue in a scooping gesture, or tickle the area softly with the finger in the same gesture. Then, during lovemaking, try positions such as the Stepping Tigers to get the right angle for the penis to reach and stimulate the G-spot.

Some women do not respond to the stimulation of this specific G-spot. If you are one of these women, this may not be where your personal G-spot actually is, and other areas of the vagina may produce more pleasure for you. Different stroking actions may be more stimulating to you, like those referred to in Sexual Reflexology and Wild Animal Positions.

But before you give up on this area entirely, I suggest trying different ways to connect to the G-spot that you may not have tried before. One would be squatting down, finding, and stroking the spot with your own finger. You can also guide your lover's penis into that area by taking the top position in coitus or while in a straddling, seated position; this will help you see how this area feels during different forms of penile contact. Enjoy playfully discovering what erotic zones, touch, pressure, and sexual positions bring you the most pleasure.

Riding High and Low

The best stimulation of the clitoris from the penis is termed "riding high." In this stroke, the penis presses against the clitoris and the front wall of the vagina for added clitoral arousal on each stroke. Use the Wrestling Monkeys and Cleaving Cicadas positions to ride high.

Riding low is the penile stroke of pressing against the back, or bottom wall, of the vagina on each stroke. This can be an innovative stroke for you that will bring you to a new dimension of sexual pleasure. Use the Soaring Phoenix sexual position mentioned earlier to ride low.

The Male G-spot Stroke

The "G-spot" for a man is the term used for the prostate gland. The male G-spot can be stimulated by pressing with the finger on the perineum point—found between the scrotum and the anus—or through actual anal stimulation by placing the index finger about three inches inside the anal canal and then making scooping or flittering actions upwards. These two stimulating strokes of the prostate gland can heighten a man's excitement and sexual endurance.

This stimulation accompanied with vaginal intercourse is incredibly arousing to the man, yet it can also help him strengthen his ability to withhold ejaculation.

Nine Shallow and One Deep Stroking

This classic Taoist stroking technique stimulates the sides of the vagina and penis for great pleasure and health benefits. The essence of the nine shallow and one deep thrusting technique is for the penis to penetrate nine shallow times into the vagina, followed by one deep thrust.

Here's how:

1. The nine shallow thrusts should be made slowly for the best results, alternating at different angles toward the walls of the vagina as well as straight in.
2. This angle of penetration offers stimulation to the reflexology zones of the vagina and penis, including the vagina's G-spot.
3. One deep thrust straight in follows to vary the sensory stimulation and reach more heightened pleasure.

4. The penis never exits the vagina completely, but withdraws to the very outer edges, which are incredible sensitive due to the nerve endings there.

5. The change in different thrusts is exhilarating and pleasurable to both lovers.

6. The female lover can relax her vaginal muscles, then grip them using the Creating the Sexual Elixir technique around the penis on any of the strokes for additional pleasure for both lovers.

7. Recommendation: three to nine sets.

Deep and Still

A deep penetration by the penis to the back of the vagina, followed by holding that position in total stillness for up to a minute, can stir a woman's arousal and make her move her hips and body wildly as well as bring a man to the point of ecstatic orgasm. The back of the vagina is an incredible pleasure spot that can bring both lovers into the place beyond mind and body. This stroke can best be performed with the woman on her stomach and the man on top. The woman can also use her fingers to stimulate her clitoris at the same time. (Her lover is welcome to join in too!)

He Spirals

This thrusting technique involves making a variety of small circles at the entrance, middle, and deeper part of the vagina.

1. The man slowly inserts his penis into his lover's vagina.

2. Once he enters, the man makes three circles in one direction at the entrance of the vagina.

3. Then he makes three circles in the opposite direction.

4. The penis thrusts into the middle of the vagina, repeating three circles in one direction and then three circles in the opposite direction.

5. The penetration moves on to the deepest part of the vagina, where the same circle technique is repeated—three circles in one direction and then three circles in the other.

These circles stimulate a woman's cool, watery nature to her boiling point. A man can vary the sequence from shallow circles to deep circles and then back to circles in the middle area of the vagina to send energy through the penis and vagina up to the vital organs and body.

She Spirals

The female partner can also make circles with her pelvis, accompanied by a contraction of the vaginal walls, while the male remains still.

1. The woman moves her pelvis in circles as many times as she desires, first in one direction while gently contracting the vagina, then relaxing her vaginal contraction as in the Breath of Pleasure.

2. She moves her pelvis in the opposite direction while she contracts the vaginal muscles, then opens up as in the Breath of Pleasure.

3. Vary the position between shallow circles, midpoint circles, and deep circles throughout the stroke.

This technique can drive both the woman and her lover wild!

Moment-to-Moment Bliss

Being present moment to moment during lovemaking allows us to enjoy the fullest pleasure of a Sacred Love-Making experience. Bringing our full self into the sexual experience can create a deep and magical event for both lovers.

What does being present feel like during lovemaking?

Presence is a state of mindfulness. When we are present during lovemaking, we are alert, attentive, and receptive to the moment and to our partner. When we are present, we experience heightened emotions and pleasure that bring excitement, aliveness, and revitalization. Presence creates a real connection and rich intimacy. Being present during lovemaking can also put us in touch with our spirit and bring about a cathartic transformation.

Disappearing

Our desiring nature (from wanting new possessions to a different sexual experience), feelings of pressure about performance, and personal aversions to love and sex can often create distractions in us during lovemaking. This usually happens when we are afraid of facing our own feelings of fear or inadequacy, or we are even afraid of a new threshold of experiencing pleasure, love, and union. We can go through the motions of sexual engagement and wonder why we are bored and discontented and have lifeless sex. Be careful of letting sex slip into a mindless routine and falling into a tendency to fantasize or to become distracted during sex. This could progressively lead to emotional isolation and sexual interest moving elsewhere.

We can deceive ourselves into believing there is something more erotic or important than what is happening in the present moment. These tendencies can easily throw a couple out of emotional harmony and sexual sync, which denies them both access to deeper levels of pleasure and ecstasy.

Sex is so much more fulfilling when we stay present in the moment. Being present in a sexual experience with our lover is a commitment to our partner, our lovemaking, and our bliss.

The Art of Love teaches us that when we have difficulty being present, we can learn to guide ourselves to reconnect through our senses. We can use visual, scent, and touch connection to bring our awareness into the present moment with our lover. As we learn to utilize our senses as connectors to the moment, it gets easier to engage in the present.

The next exercise invites you to become more attuned to your partner through being present moment to moment. These suggestions will also help attune you more skillfully to the subtle arts of creating and partaking of the sexual elixir during lovemaking.

Be Present Moment to Moment:

- Be aware of your lover.

- Look into each other's eyes.

- Watch the expressions on your partner's face.

- Feel the movements and actions that bring your partner pleasure.

- Listen to your partner's breathing and notice his or her state of arousal.

- Smell your lover's scent.

- Taste your lover's tongue, mouth, and body.

- Notice your lover's emotions.

- Notice your own emotions as you make love with your partner.

- Use all of your senses—hearing, scent, taste, touch, sight, and your sixth sense of intuition—to enjoy this sacred moment even more fully.

SACRED LOVE-MAKING
unites you and your lover physically, emotionally, mentally and spiritually.

Partaking of the Sexual Elixir

Many of the world's religious rituals use food and drink as the symbol of communing with the divine. Partaking of the Sexual Elixir is also utilized in this way, offering the sustenance of vital energy and love to feed the sacred communion of your intimate relationship. Partaking of the sexual elixir is the art of directing the sexual elixir to the whole body to nurture and satisfy your and your lover's ultimate pleasure, well-being, and deeper union.

As you have moved through the arts to make your love more sacred and ecstatic, you have probably found that you are becoming more aware of the sexual sensations that you are creating and how they are satisfying both you and your lover. This new awareness will be vital to you now in perceiving the subtlest movements of energy that will occur internally for you and your lover during this next advanced lovemaking art.

This lovemaking art is designed for you to become comfortable and skillful at creating, partaking, and circulating your sexual elixir through your own Microcosmic Orbit during lovemaking. Both lovers can then simultaneously feel and amplify the sensational and subtle energetic alchemy taking place.

To begin create the sexual elixir. First, join in coitus and begin the movements of lovemaking with your lover. Breathe at your own pace as you focus on creating *your own* elixir. Slowly breathe. *Women*: Inhale, close the entrance of the vagina. *Men*: Inhale, close the tip of the penis while drawing up the testicles. Exhale. Repeat your individual breathing several times to create the sexual elixir. You can also breathe in unison to prepare for the next step in this lovemaking art.

Partaking of the Sexual Elixir

Step One, Up and Down the Spine
In unison, breathe into your own Sexual Palaces and:

- Begin to sip up the sexual elixir on the inhale of Creating the Sexual Elixir.
- Contract the genitals and draw the sexual elixir up to each center along the back channel of your personal Microcosmic Orbit toward the crown of your head.
- Hold the contraction and the breath at the crown.
- Exhale and relax the genital muscles.
- Draw your awareness back down your spine to the Sexual Palace.

You can either stop here or rest for a minute or more before continuing to the next level of lovemaking with the elixir. During your rest time, notice the sensations that have been produced from your sexual energy moving up and down *your own* spine during lovemaking.

Step Two, Circulate the Sexual Elixir
In unison, breathe into your own Sexual Palaces:

- Inhale the sexual elixir again to intensify it.
- Draw the sexual elixir toward the crown at the top of your head.
- Feel the sexual elixir rising into each center along your orbit.
- Hold the breath and contract for a few seconds.
- Exhale and relax.
- Let the sexual elixir flow down the front of your body like honey.
- Feel it reach the third eye between the eyebrows.
- Then let it flow through the palate at the top of the mouth, sweetening your tongue and saliva.
- Let it move through the throat center at the base of your throat and proceed toward the: Heart Center, Solar Plexus, which is the central area where the thoracic ribcages meet, to the Navel, and then back to the Sexual Palace.
- Repeat three to six times.

Feel the sensation of the sexual elixir electrifying and enlivening your body. As you sharpen this art of Partaking of the Sexual Elixir, your lovemaking will enter a new stratosphere of pleasure and fulfillment.

Partaking of Ecstasy

This sexual alchemy art produces a new playing field for a couple. It will bring you closer than you ever thought possible during sex, and this closeness will continue long after the experience has ended.

Building on Partaking of the Sexual Elixir, share the currency of the elixir flowing upwards now with your lover. In Partaking of Ecstasy, you will make one energy circulation rather than two separate, individual circulations. Your love for each other and your combined sexual elixir will become one unified force so powerful that it can awaken a crescendo of healing and ecstasy. Take your time as you move into these greater levels of sacred sharing, pleasure, and communion. Then rest and relax in blissful oneness with your Sacred Lover.

Partaking of Ecstasy
First join in coitus and begin the movements of lovemaking with your lover.

In unison, create one Sexual Elixir for both Sexual Palaces:
Slowly breathe together: *Women*: Inhale, and close the entrance of the vagina. *Men*: Inhale, and close the tip of the penis while drawing up the testicles. Both exhale.

Next, in unison, partake of the Sexual Elixir:
- Enhance the elixir as you fuse more deeply with your lover in coitus.
- Draw the sexual elixir up your own back channel to your shared crowns.
- Then let it flow down the back channel of your lover's body at the same time.
- Synchronize your breathing.
- Sip the sexual elixir through one partner's orbit first.
- Then let it flow down the back of the other partner afterwards.
- You can rest between each circulation or repeat the circulations a couple of times, then rest.
- Repeat three to nine times, creating a unified field of love, pleasure, and ecstasy together.

Note: In the beginning, you may feel that you are working to circulate your energy during lovemaking. However, after just a few times, you will use less muscle and more mind and breath power. And the more energy you can feel, the less energy rotations you will need to awaken to a state of ecstasy.

The Immortal decided to call the couple from the sanctuary into the library, as this next technique required an even greater level of concentration. She did not want her students to become distracted by the sounds of nature and the cool, late-afternoon breeze that had just come in. The room was filled with the Immortal's private collection of rare literary treasures and medicinal canons.

The Immortal gestured for the couple to come and sit by the fire so that she could share with them the wisdom of orgasmic lovemaking.

"Orgasm is considered the crowning gift of lovemaking that allows lovers to transcend the ego self and connect with the true self. While reaching one orgasm during lovemaking can be perceived as a great achievement, having two, three, or more is considered traveling beyond physical lovemaking into the realm of ultimate coupling.

"A Sacred Lover frequently enjoys multiple orgasms with his or her lover. Orgasm rises to the mountain top and descends through two spirits, two hearts, two bodies, only to begin the ascent again.

"Taoist masters consider women to be more adept at experiencing multi-orgasmic pleasure, relative to their ability to enjoy an increasing wave of pleasure rather than a diminishing of pleasure due to the loss of semen."

"How can a man experience multiple orgasms if he loses his semen?" asked the male student.

"A man can develop his ability to withhold and redirect ejaculation to experience multiple orgasms. Multi-orgasmic pleasure in both women and men is experienced as waves of energy and pleasure that move inwards and upwards. Each wave builds, one on top of another, surpassing a short, pleasurable pulsating release.

"A man can tune into his feminine counterpart's pleasure during lovemaking to easily learn how to reach a state of multiple orgasm."

"Are we to focus on our own pleasure building or our partner's during this art?" asked the woman.

"Both," replied the teacher. "Although it takes individual skill to execute this art, the close play of supporting and guiding the energy between you and your lover is essential to a multi-orgasmic lovemaking experience for both lovers. With practice, each lover can simultaneously support and enhance the other's enjoyment of reaching multiple orgasms."

Reaching Multi-Orgasmic Lovemaking

An orgasmic experience can bring forth significant pleasure. Through the prior arts of Sacred Love-Making you have most probably enjoyed at least one satisfying orgasm. Incorporating these lovemaking arts helps those who have had difficulty achieving orgasm experience the satisfaction that they have long desired. These arts also significantly expand the feelings of pleasure to those who are already orgasmic.

So why does one need to experience more orgasms? Multiple orgasms are very pleasing and can satisfy you and your partner in a new way. While one orgasm can give you the feeling of finality, having multiple orgasms offers a journey of wave after wave of heightened gratification. While this alone is an amazing addition to your lovemaking, there is also something else. Through achieving the art of multiple orgasms you can begin to experience what it feels like to be one with the universe.

Orgasmic energy is the very state of life itself; it is our true essence. All life forms are created through orgasm. Our universe pulsates with orgasmic creativity, and our cells pulsate with this original fertile bliss. By learning to become multi-orgasmic you not only enjoy more pleasure and satisfaction, you can also become more in tune with the powerful beauty and divine rhythm of the universe. To do this, you only have to remember your innate ability to vibrate with orgasmic pleasure and life-giving ecstatic energy.

Multiple orgasms are created from three sexual alchemy ingredients. First, you have to activate a very high sexual arousal state, close to the point of orgasm. Secondly, you need to Partake of the Sexual Elixir by sipping the sexual energy up to the crown of the head. Then you will need to add one last important ingredient.

When the top of the mountain and the bottom of the sea engage, multiple orgasms are set in motion. This is code for the important last ingredient, "the power lock." The power lock is a combination of different muscle groups utilized to activate the sacral pump, located at the bottom of the spine, and the cranial pump, located at the top of the spine. You can instantly feel a pleasure current rising rapidly when you activate the lock; this process will be detailed in the following pages. When you "power lock," your two pumps quickly draw the sexual energy upwards toward the brain instead of outwards into male ejaculation or female exhaustion.

This power lock can help you both create multiple orgasms.

Orgasms are then experienced moving upwards rather than outwards, allowing the opportunity for more than one. The power lock empowers both individuals in developing their capacity for greater pleasure and also to share even more orgasmic and ecstatic pleasure with each other during lovemaking.

Women develop greater orgasmic sensitivity by activating arousal to create the sexual elixir. Then they can utilize the power lock to draw their orgasmic energy up the spine. Women can ride the waves of sexual arousal upwards to enjoy repeated orgasmic experiences during lovemaking.

Men, too, can become multi-orgasmic by utilizing the power lock. Men can experience greater pleasure and lovemaking longevity by moving their pleasure upwards. With continued practice of this art, a man can also separate the experience of orgasm from ejaculation. When this is possible, a man will feel more empowered to consciously delay the time before ejaculation or not to ejaculate at all during a lovemaking experience.

Activating a multi-orgasmic experience can bring you heightened enjoyment and ecstatic bliss. Bringing yourself and your partner into this blissful state during lovemaking by utilizing the power lock is a profound relationship gift.

The Art of Multiple Orgasms

This art builds on the prior Sacred Love-Making arts. Both partners will cultivate the sexual elixir together to a heightened state. Right before orgasm, each partner will sip the sexual elixir to the crown of the head while utilizing the defining multi-orgasmic tool, the power lock.

The power lock utilizes different areas of the body to activate the sacral and cranial pumps. Remember, these two physical/energy pumps can quickly, at the point prior to orgasm, draw the sexual elixir upwards toward the crown instead of outwards into ejaculation and exhaustion.

Practice the Power Lock

Give yourself ample practice with the power lock alone prior to performing it during lovemaking:

1. Curl the toes under.
2. Tighten the buttocks and thighs.
3. Close the fists.
4. Bring the chin in.
5. Swallow up toward the crown.
6. As you draw your sexual energy upwards toward the crown of the head, the eyes will also roll upwards toward the crown.
7. Then relax all the muscles.

Reach Heightened Arousal for Multiple Orgasms
Start by arousing yourself to between 50 to 60 percent of capacity. Create the elixir.

For Women:
The Tao says women take longer to heat up, but once they do, they can go forever. Women tend to feel multiple orgasms more quickly and can increase their level of pleasure immensely through this practice. (Note: do not practice while on your period or in cases of bladder or vaginal infections.)

Begin by stimulating yourself:

- Touch your breast or genital area.
- Gently breathe in.
- Close the vagina with your mind and a little muscle.
- Exhale, let it open, and relax.

For Men:
This practice will help you separate orgasm from ejaculation to be able to delay or stop ejaculation. Effectively using the power lock will bring the sexual energy up the spine into orgasm instead of out the penis into ejaculation. This process takes practice. When you feel you are getting close to ejaculation, contract the perineum muscles and pull the sexual energy up the spine to experience orgasm within your body instead of ejaculating and experiencing an outer orgasm.

Begin by stimulating yourself:

- Touch your body or genital area or both.
- Gently breathe in and close the tip of the penis.
- Draw up the testicles.
- Exhale. Let these areas relax.
- Then draw the sexual elixir to the crown of the head with your breath and the power lock.
- Work up to a 75, then 85 percent arousal point.
- Practice the upward draw again.

(Note: only proceed to a more heightened arousal state once you have felt successful with the previous.)

Multi-Orgasmic Lovemaking

Join in coitus:

- As you make love, each partner will become more and more aroused.
- As each partner reaches the point before orgasm, Partake of the Sexual Elixir while utilizing the power lock.

Both of you:

- Curl the toes.
- Turn your tailbone under.
- Lock the chin.
- Tighten the thighs and buttocks.
- Clench the fists.
- Swallow up as you draw the sexual elixir to the top of the head.
- Hold the breath at the crown until you feel the sexual elixir traveling away from the genitals and up to the brain.
- Then exhale and relax.
- Feel the energy wave of orgasm all over your body.
- Share the orgasmic wave by allowing it to flow between you and your lover.
- Repeat the sequence.
- Build your arousal again by making love.
- Draw the pre-orgasmic energy up to the crown.
- Hold your breath until the elixir moves up.
- Then exhale and relax into bliss.
- Give and receive orgasmic energy with each other.
- Enjoy orgasmic pleasure, joy, and ecstasy building and lengthening.
- Safely store the energy from this practice in the dantien by circling the hands at the area below the navel.
- Then rest, enjoy, and relax.

Note for men:

Men can choose either to ejaculate after practicing or not to ejaculate at all. Utilize your own best judgment when cultivating this art. As a man, it is important to your development of these ancient Taoist lovemaking methods to recognize that it is okay not to ejaculate during or at the end of every self-pleasuring and lovemaking experience.

Progress at your own pace. Learning how to bring the aroused sexual elixir up rather than out is a process. Continue to draw the sexual orgasmic energy up when you are close to orgasm. If you utilize this art correctly, you will be able to move your sexual energy that would usually become semen into a reinvigorating tonic and pleasure potion for you and your lover. This art will help you expand the experience of orgasm and ride the wave of multiple orgasms.

Orgasmic Continuum

As you lie together with your partner after multi-orgasmic lovemaking, feel your heart energy merging with your partner's heart energy. You will perpetuate the love and pleasure experience of multi-orgasmic lovemaking, which can now expand even more.

Safely Storing Orgasmic Energy

After lovemaking, always direct the sexual energy back to the area underneath the navel with your mind and by smiling down to this area. The dantien will safely hold energy and release chi like a time capsule to parts of your body that need healing or more vital energy when they need them.

As the Immortal was coming to the climax of the story, a bolt of lightening appeared in the sky. She laughed and said, "It looks like rain.

"Bedroom artists consider this mystical lovemaking practice the culminating Elixir of Sacred Love-Making. The body merges with spirit. Matter becomes identical with source. The couple experiences the weaving of concurrent polarities: duality and oneness, fullness and emptiness, heaven and earth. With cultivation of this practice, if they so desire, they can access the secrets of the universe."

"Is this practice more important than the one before?" asked the man.

"Each lovemaking practice has its own significance and is appropriate for different couples at different times. If a couple is drawn to and engages in this spiritual lovemaking practice it will offer great benefits for love, pleasure, and mystical intoxication."

A thunderbolt boomed as golden precipitation showered down.

"It's time for rain," said the Immortal as she took the couple to dance with her in the light rain.

Sacred Love-Making

Are you ready to travel to the highest heights and know the deepest of connections with your lover during sex?

During this Sacred Love-Making journey, you have been exposed to many possibilities to enrich your love life. Now consider this: What if it were possible to energetically merge as one with your partner and experience the universe simultaneously? Or expand your heart and sexual openness and experience an enlightened orgasm? If so, this next art is for you.

This lovemaking art can widen your vision of ecstasy and offer you the experience of transcendental sexuality. You can enjoy the intensity of multi-orgasmic lovemaking while simultaneously experiencing spiritual awakening and ecstatic oneness with your lover.

Orgasm releases the spirit into its natural awakened state of ecstasy. Consciously adding the spiritual dimension to your lovemaking will bring deeper love and fulfillment to your sexual relationship.

We can achieve a state of transcendence through sex by first developing our own sensitivity to subtle body energies and cosmic energies. This level of connection depends most importantly on your personal level of Sacred Lover cultivation that I have discussed throughout this book.

Sacred Love-Making takes place through the interaction of two developed Sacred Lovers sharing the same intention for conscious sex. This desire builds the energy field for the experience to take place. Then, when Yin and Yang have intertwined, the polarization of male and female is transcended, and two lovers can merge in unity with the ultimate.

We have learned in previous chapters to bring the sexual elixir up toward the crown of the head, the center of spiritual enlightenment. As you bring this energy up to the crown, you will begin to activate your spiritual connection by spiraling your spiritual energy on the crown of the head. You will circle it first in one direction, and then back in the opposite direction. Then you will bring this blended sexual and spiritual energy above the head and body and spiral it first in one direction and then the other.

You will then experience two things; first, your sexual orgasmic energy will expand up and mushroom into an orb around your and your lover's bodies. This stage represents a state of merging with your lover's spirit. Second, you may have the sensation that the boundaries and separation of physical bodies has dissolved between you and your partner. In this divine moment, you can feel bliss and awareness of the meaning of life—the experience of oneness with everything. Your consciousness can be transformed in an instant. This orgasmic state can last hours or even days after the lovemaking experience.

The ego seeks control and fears dissolution, so be patient. It may take six months to two years or even longer to work into this spiritual state of rapture. The ego will increasingly let go the safer it feels with the partner you have chosen and with the ultimate sexual experience overall. As you practice, let more passion and lovemaking skills unfold organically. Relax and enjoy the journey of Sacred Love.

This experience of embodying the divine essence of life during the sexual experience is the true intention of Sacred Love. It requires commitment, love, and respect. This process will help you let go of wounds, fears, and disconnectedness. Allow this lovemaking to reinvigorate your union and feed your spirit. Notice a deeper connection with your loved one, with nature, and with the infinite universe. It is a journey of love.

Sacred Love-Making Experience

- Make love.
- Each partner contracts the genitals and sips the sexual elixir to the crown on one inhale.
- Hold at the crown and spiral the elixir around both crowns.
- Count to nine slowly.
- Exhale.
- Allow the elixir to expand up above the crown and out from the bodies.
- Feel the orgasm rising up through your body, heart, and head, awakening your spirit.
- Feel the bliss of sharing this joy with your partner.
- Let the elixir rain down around both lovers to experience sexual and spiritual bliss in the physical as well as your subtle spiritual bodies that you can't see, but may perceive.
- Repeat the sequence three to six times.
- Feel simultaneously grounded and suspended in spiritual, sexual ecstasy.
- Relax and feel the ecstasy flowing through you both.

Fountain of Bliss

- Feel the orgasmic energy now rising up through the center of your body, heart, and head, fully awakening your sexuality, heart, and spirit.
- Spiral the elixir around both crowns nine times.

- Now feel the Sexual Spiritual Elixir expanding beyond both bodies.
- Exhale and smile.
- Allow the energy to spread out and rain down around both bodies.
- Feel yourself merging with your lover, nature, and the infinite universe.
- Feel the bliss of sacred fusion on all levels.
- Repeat the sequence three to six times.
- Rest in sublime unity.

At times, you may experience hours of orgasmic ecstasy flowing through your body and between you and your Sacred Lover, long after any of these lovemaking arts have finished.

Remember to practice mindful care and safety by bringing the sexual energy back to the dantien underneath the navel when you are finished. Rest and enjoy the love and the sexual and spiritual sacredness of your lovemaking experience. Taste immortality.

Surrendering to Ecstasy and Ultimate Love

When she has let go of herself she is perfectly fulfilled.
 —Lao Tzu

Surrender takes the highest level of courage. Allowing ourselves to receive the ecstatic pleasure that is taking place in the moment of lovemaking calls for a great deal of trust.

It is a representation of the Yin skills we possess. Surrendering during Sacred Love-Making is the process of relaxing into the ecstasy you have created during lovemaking, dissolving your ego, and opening to the wonders of the universe.

Roots and Wings

Lovers can hold the space of love and support for each other that create an anchor to expand their consciousness and surrender. When this anchor is in place, both lovers have the trust to enable them to take flight.

The male enters all of himself into the female to then expand and become united with all that is. The female opens all of herself to the male to expand infinitely. Your availability and willingness to be this present and open is defined by strength and vulnerability at the same time.

Surrendering during Sacred Love-Making allows us to feel ourselves as fully as we are capable. We can experience the pulsations of ecstasy in our tiniest of cells and in the ecstatic awakening of our bodies, hearts, minds, and spirits. Feel the energy buzzing—feel the ecstasy of going deep into each other's hearts, bodies, and souls. Surrender brings us to divine pleasure and our own greatest experience of being.

Integrating

Sacred Love-Making integrates you more lovingly with yourself and your lover, and nurtures your connection with pure awareness.

Whether for minutes or hours, depending on the particular lovemaking experience, you can enjoy unbounded ecstasy and oneness integrating you and your lover. Savor the sublime pulsations of Sacred Love naturally coursing through your being after lovemaking has finished. Experience the effects of transformation. Allow your Sacred Love-Making experience to continue to nurture and deepen the integrity and wholeness of your intimate relationship.

Enjoy a Lifetime of Passion and Sacred Love

Cherish bringing the sacred into your lovemaking. Each Sacred Love-Making experience enriches your connection to love, pleasure, and intimate union.

I encourage you to develop your ability as a love artist by cultivating the Sacred Lover in you, practicing the Talent of Loving Another, and exploring the Art of Sacred Love-Making to experience the profound gifts that sacred love and lovemaking can offer you.

Utilize this book daily to continually renew and enrich your love life. Or you can refer to this book as regularly as you need or desire.

These skills, talents, and arts can have a profound and life-changing effect on your intimate evolution. They can offer you and your lover true and abundant joy, wholeness, and intimate fulfillment for a lifetime.

As the day's lessons had come to a close, the female illu-minate gathered the couples in the garden to see the beau-tiful sunset. She bowed to them, and they bowed back to her. She asked each to close their eyes so she could lead them through a silent meditation.

When the students opened their eyes, they felt a gentle breeze caressing their cheeks, which indicated that their teacher had left. If they had by chance looked out toward the sunset, they could still catch a glimpse of her disap-pearing into the horizon, returning to the jade pond, the abode of Immortals.

Music Suggestions Appendix

Objects of Desire/A Sensual Compilation—The Best of Blush Records, Vol. #1

Under the Lover's Moon by Ken Kritzberg

From the Choirgirl Hotel by Tori Amos

Sky Kisses Earth by Prem Joshua

Shri Durga by DJ Cheb I. Sabbah

Love's Divine by Seal

Sacred Love by Sting

Ray of Light by Madonna

Embrace by Deva Premal

Baduizm by Erykah Badu

Acoustic Soul by India Arie

Luther Vandross: Greatest Hits by Luther Vandross

Barry White—All-Time Greatest Hits by Barry White

Life Blood by Joanne Shenandoah (with Peter Kater)

Shiva Station by Jai Uttal

Diaspora by Natacha Atlas

Portals of Grace by Azam Ali

Bibliography

Stephen Mitchell Translation, Tao Te Ching-Lao Tzu, Harper Collins, New York, 1999

Riane Eisler, *Chalice and the Blade*, Harper Collins, New York, 1987

Riane Eisler, *Sacred Pleasure*, Harper Collins, New York 1996

Deepak Chopra and Fereydoun Kia, *The Love Poems of Rumi*, Harmony Books: New York, 1998

Thomas Cleary, *Immortal Sisters, Secret Teachings of Taoist Women*, Shambhala: Boston, 1989

Jeanne Elizabeth Blum, *Woman Heal Thyself*, Charles E Tuttle Co., Inc.: Boston, 1995

Dr. Stephen T. Chang, *The Tao of Sexology*, Tao Publishing, Nevada,1986

Robert Ornstein, PhD, and David Sobel, MD, *Healthy Pleasures*, Perseus Books: New York, 1998

Valentin Chu, *The Yin-Yang Butterfly*, Jeremy P. Tarcher/Putnam: New York, 1994

Nik Douglas and Penny Slinger, *Sexual Secrets, The Alchemy of Ecstasy*, Destiny Books: Vermont 1979

Lauren Slater, "This Thing Called Love," *National Geographic,* The National Geographic Society: Washington D.C., February 2006

Mantak Chia and Maneewan Chia, Douglas Abrams, and Rachel Carlton Abrams, MD, *The Multi-Orgasmic Couple*, Harper: San Francisco, 2000

Mantak Chia and Maneewan Chia, *Cultivating Female Sexual Energy*, Healing Tao Press: New York, 1986

Mantak Chia and Michael Winn, *Taoist Secrets of Love*, Aurora Press: New York, 1984

Jalaja Bonheim, PhD, *The Hunger for Ecstasy*, DayBreak-Rodale Books: New York, 2001

Napoleon Hill, *Think and Grow Rich*, Hawthorne Books, 1972

Sri Sri Ravi Shankar, *Creating Silence*, Art of Living Foundation, 2001

Muriel Rukeyser, "Looking at Each Other" in *Love in Praise and Celebration*, Helen Exley, Exley Publications, New York, 1995

Rumi, "Show me your Face" Nadir Khalili, *Fountain of Fire*, Cal Earth Press, California, 1994

Genesis and Song of Solomon, King James Version-Parallel Bible, Zondervan: Michigan, 1995

I invite you to visit our Web site at
www.SacredLove.com
to discover:

- **Even More Meaningful Intimacy Insights and Products**
- **Frequently Asked Questions**
- **The Upcoming Schedule of Teleseminars, Media Appearances, Speaking Engagements, and Seminars with Karinna Kittles-Karsten**

If you would like to learn more about the Fit for Love exercises mentioned throughout Intimate Wisdom, see the *Fit for Love* e-book and audio workout series package at www.sacredlove.com and take advantage of your free download offer on the next page.

www.SacredLove.com

Free Audio Download Offer

As my way of saying thanks for buying this book, I am pleased to offer you one of the following downloads from the www.sacredlove.com collection at no charge to you. I would also like to ask a small request. If this book has touched, helped, or inspired you, please tell your friends about it.

Check one Audio Download you'd like:

❑ Fit for Love, Part One, Opening the Body to Love
❑ Fit for Love, Part Two, Increasing Sexual Vitality and Sexual Healing
❑ Fit for Love, Part Three, Opening to Pleasure and Ecstasy
❑ Healthy Sexuality

Please Print Clearly

Name:_____

Address: _____

City: _____ State: _____ Zip: _____

Phone: (_____) _____

E-mail: _____ (you will be contacted by e-mail)

No phone orders will be accepted.
You can E-mail this form to info@sacredlove.com;
Fax this form to: 310-230-9848;
Or mail it to:
Sacred Love
PO Box 1371
Pacific Palisades, Ca 90272

Are you interested in improving an existing relationship? _____
Are you looking for "the one"? _____

*As an added bonus, you will receive my free monthly Sacred Love e-newsletter, plus the weekly "Ask Karinna" column from www.sacredlove.com.

A Gift for Singles

<u>**Four Important Questions to Ask Yourself**</u>
<u>**Before Having Sex for the First Time with Someone**</u>

1-Do you know him or her? How well do you know this person and for how long?

2-Is he/she healthy? Do you know his/her sexual health status?

3-How's your self-esteem right now? Are you honoring yourself emotionally, mentally, physically and spiritually and the other person by making this choice? And will you love yourself by having this sexual experience? Before having sex? During sex? After having sex?

4-Are you in your right mind? Are you under the influence of intoxicants that would prevent you making the right choice?

For further information, go to www.sacredlove.com.

Note: You may want to cut this out as a reminder to carry with you in your purse or wallet to help you always make the right choice for you.

978-0-595-41957-9
0-595-41957-7

Printed in the United States
139834LV00003B/138/A